SUE WAF

HORARY AST
ABDUCTION & MURDER
THE HORARY METHOD APPLIED TO 16 CASES

PRISMA
EDIÇÕES

HORARY ASTROLOGY: ABDUCTION & MURDER
The Horary Method Applied to 16 Cases

Author: Sue Ward
Design: João Xavier
Cover Illustration: João Xavier

ISBN: 979-8355355098

Coleção Academia de Astrologia
1st Edition / 2022

Prisma Edições
www.prismaedicoes.com

Contents

Abbreviations

ANPR   Automatic Number Plate Recognition [camera]
BST   British Summer Time
CCTV   Closed-Circuit Television
CEST   Central European Summer Time
DNA   Deoxyribonucleic Acid [genetic identifier]
DVD   Digital Versatile Disk
GMT   Greenwich Mean Time
IC   *Imum Coeli* [Bottom of the Sky]
MC   *Medium Coeli* [Midheaven]
PDT   Pacific Daylight Time
UK   United Kingdom

HORARY ASTROLOGY: ABDUCTION & MURDER
The Horary Method Applied to 16 Cases

PREFACE

It is commonly understood that knowledge is power; knowledge can help to heal; knowledge can help us to understand tragedy.

I have thought long and hard about writing a book such as this; since my first lecture on this subject in 1996, people have pressed me to write this book. My reticence has been two-fold: I am lazy and writing books is hard work; and the subject matter is sensitive and needs careful handling. I would not want to be party to a ghoulish sort of 'rubber-necking'. The intention here is to offer an informal insight into the workings of the chart in extreme circumstances. It will also emphasize the weight of the astrologer's responsibility. Perhaps one day we will become so good at judging charts such as these that the police will feel able to trust us, so such experience might be useful.

In order to introduce some sensitivity into these proceedings, I will not give the full names of victims in most cases. These are mostly well-known cases and can be easily found. But it seems to me that there is no point in running the risk of causing any more suffering to the families of victims, or to the victims themselves. I will also be taking a rather detached approach for what I think are obvious reasons. You will find two charts that are not of abductions but I hope that will not detract from their interest.

The charts are included in chronological order because there did not seem to be another way of ordering them. You will notice that many are old, but forensic science has progressed massively in that time, particularly DNA profiling, resulting in the successful conclusion of many such cases. Although there are no horaries in this collection, the same techniques are applied to the various event and inception charts. The same perspective is required, that of making enquiry of the astrological figure.

The cases presented here are to demonstrate the method I use; they do not have a strictly didactic purpose. I assume that you will read through in order, thus something that I have explained in one chart will not necessarily be explained subsequently. If you want to know more about the methods I employ, please see my textbook *Sue Ward's Traditional Horary Course* and *Christian Astrology* by William Lilly (1602-1681).

I am sure that you will be able to find arguments that, for one reason or another, I have not commented upon, but it would be true to say that we would each find a different, but similar, route through the many arguments contained in these charts. And you may find occasional errors and I ask your forgiveness for that – perfection takes a little longer!

PRECEPTS

The Fundamentals

In the first place, I assume that you will have some understanding of the traditional system and method and therefore I will not explain the various techniques that are applied in the following charts. Should you require definitions or explanations, as already mentioned, I suggest you refer to my textbook *Sue Ward's Traditional Horary Course*, or *Christian Astrology* by William Lilly where you will find everything that you need.

My education in astrology is largely in the tradition found in the early modern period and somewhat precedent to that. I work within the early modern tradition and so all of my arguments here derive from that method. It is from William Lilly's work that I have learnt almost all of what I know about astrology in practice and theory, and will be applying that here, although without references. As mentioned, in this book I have no didactic ambitions, it is purely for demonstration purposes.

I shall comment on the Part of Death in most cases because I have always used it in these matters. The calculation is that from al-Biruni as the 8th cusp plus Saturn minus the Moon.[1] There are others.

You will notice my frequent use of the five-degree rule: when a planet is within five degrees of a house cusp, it is counted as if it were in the subsequent house. It is a common traditional principle.

I have provided Ptolemy's Table of Essential Dignities and some other tabulated information that you might find useful as you study the enclosed charts.

---

1 . Abu'l-Rayhan Muhammad ibn Ahmad al-Biruni, *The Book of Instruction in the Elements of the Art of Astrology*, trans. R. Ramsay Wright (London, 1934), p. 286.

The Significant Moment

This has to be discussed to ensure that there is some clarity about what this means particularly in the ensuing contexts. I should first explain the difference in astrology that I perceive between an event and an inception even though they may appear to be the same and are treated the same. In the former, we might consider an earthquake or other natural catastrophe, or a train crash for example, to be an event. The astrologer might take the time, if known, of that event in order to try to understand it and perhaps to see what might come of it. The inception on the other hand implies a degree of control or intention, where a choice has been exercised which is not apparent in any other kind of event. It is of course, an event in itself but as I shall explain there is a marked difference in the quality of those significant moments in the current context.

There are few, if any, occasions when there is only one significant moment, and deciding when a beginning has occurred is equally fraught. The beginning of a baby's life is its birth; or is it its conception; or is it when its parents met; or is it when its grandparents met? You see what I mean. But we might side step this conundrum by dealing with the 'immediate' inception, as we do when we investigate the nativity to describe the events of a child's life. When a person does not return home when expected, there are a number of courses of action that the family or loved ones might pursue. These days, the first course is to try to call them on their mobile telephone. The second might be to contact someone at the place they were last known to be; their workplace or school, for example. The next course might be to telephone friends to try to locate that person. Usually, it is a last resort to call the police and report the person as missing, and consequently, this is almost always the most important time, although it can be superseded by the next common significant moment. The report is an inception because an element of choice and decision-making is required.

The time that the person was last seen is also important as an event rather than as an inception, but these must be confirmed sightings. There are instances when this time might serve as an inception for example when the person has decided to return home, go to work, or some other activity. It would be an event if someone just happened to see the person. This discussion does not really affect the astrology but might help us to decide which significant moment is more significant than another. Clearly, the reported time, if it can be obtained, is exact since the police always log all calls exactly;

when a person is last seen can be vague or inaccurate. Sometimes, there is no alternative but to use the time that the person, or their body, is discovered.

The chart that I find least helpful is the horary. You might find it odd that a horary astrologer should say that, but there are a number of variables involved in any horary chart. If the question comes from someone who is closely involved with the matter, then it can be considered. A horary question such as 'where is he?' is surely encompassed in the reported missing time. The latter is a time where the matter is pressing hard on the minds of the loved ones and few people will make that call except under duress, although there is an example here which contradicts that. Still, removing the inherent emotion of the horary question is, in my view, helpful.

Most information comes from news outlets and these might be less than exact when reporting times; a recent report was cited as being at 7.25 am when, in fact, it occurred at 7.26 am. This makes little difference to the astrology but sometimes the times given are wide of the mark: 'just after 1 pm'; 'a little before lunchtime'. The earliest media reports tend to be the most detailed because journalists will be scraping around for information and are more likely to report absolutely everything they have. It has come to my notice lately that it seems that it is the tabloids that carry additional information much earlier than the broadsheets. I will not speculate on the reasons for that but it is always advisable to accumulate a variety of sources where possible.

Moving into the modern age, there are far more opportunities for accurate timings from the swathe of CCTV and ANPR cameras used by the police for monitoring traffic. Then there is electronic technology, especially mobile telephones for accurate locations. Another crucial factor in modern investigations is DNA processing which has progressed enormously in recent years.

To sum up, there may be a number of significant moments, but in my view the most important are the last seen and the reported missing times. There are sometimes others found in a number of the examples herein. Obviously, too many and you will become confused but as always the final arbiter is description which may not always be easy to find, but you must find it.

Emma

With this case there is one event chart and two inceptions, although there might be some argument about the first.

Emma was an eleven-year-old who had been visiting her grandmother who had been ill; her uncle sent her to the shop to get something he needed to cook a meal. It was discovered in recent years that the shop had closed early because of a blizzard – they had denied this at the time of the investigation, so Emma's journey was wasted. She had made arrangements to meet friends for a trip to the cinema; this seems to have been the reason for her deciding to catch the bus instead of returning to her grandmother's house. She was never seen again, her body has never been found, and no-one has ever been charged with her disappearance.

Last seen
23 February 1957, 4.15 pm GMT
55°N53', 4°W15'

This time is usually given as 4.15 pm GMT but could have been 4.10 pm when she left her grandmother's house; a sign of long ascension rises and so there is only a marginal difference astrologically between the two times. So the Sun as ruler of the Ascendant is Emma's significator which is in the 7th house and very close to the 8th house cusp. Emma is moving towards danger. The Moon is about to change signs indicating that a change is impending, which might well be describing the fact that she was going to board a bus in about thirty-five minutes' time. But before that change occurs the Moon completes its mutual application to square Jupiter – the short journey to reach her friends, but Jupiter is not benefic here. It is detrimented, retrograde,

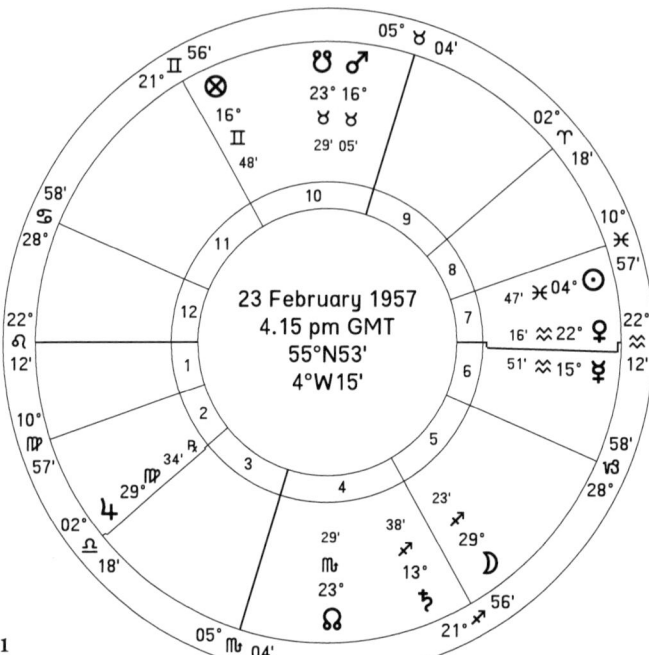

Figure 1.1
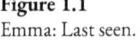
Emma: Last seen.

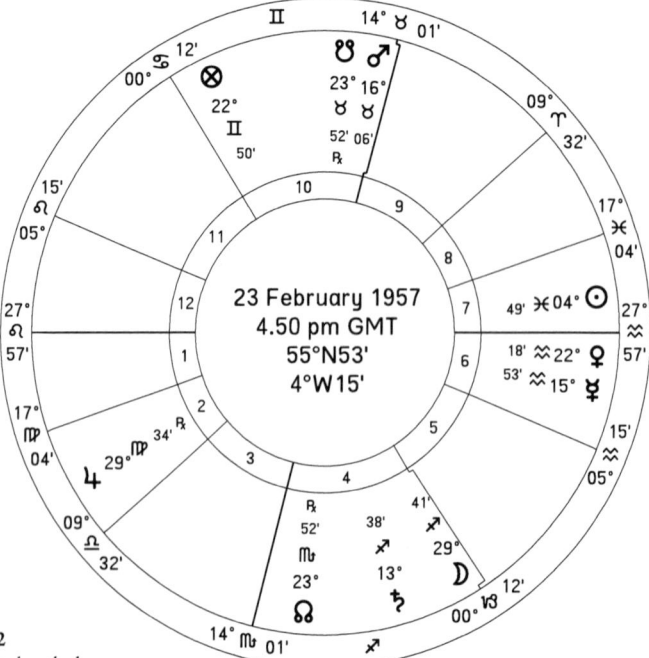

Figure 1.2
Emma: Catches the bus.

cadent, and ruler of the unfortunate 8th house; it disposits Emma's significator. The suddenness of the mutual application perhaps indicating Emma's sudden decision not to return to her grandmother's house; the Moon rules the 12th and with Jupiter's poor condition indicates a bad decision. In this combination, it is notable that Jupiter rules the 8th house and it is this aspect that prevents her from completing her errand and returning. The Moon will enter its detriment in Capricorn.

The malefics are involved, in this case because they are angular and the Sun is in square to Saturn (it could be argued that the Sun and Mars are just about in a sextile aspect) closely involved with the 7th house and dispositor of the Part of Death at about 15° Aquarius. The Part of Death can provide a motive and/or a cause of death. Saturn whilst being the natural ruler of death is also significant of suffocation as a cause of death. The angularity of the malefics in this context is ominous, and it is rare that they are not closely involved in such situations, as you will notice in the following cases.

Mercury and Venus are also angular and note must be taken of that, and both are disposited by Saturn, natural ruler of death and ruler of the 7th house of an attacker/abductor. Venus and Mars being angular introduce a sexual atmosphere that is reinforced by their being in aspect.

Catches the bus
23 February 1957, 4.50 pm GMT
Coordinates as above

There are a number of witnesses to Emma boarding this bus and that she was the only passenger. Being a conscious decision, unlike the previous chart, this is an inception.

The astrology has not changed a great deal except that the Ascendant is now in late degrees which, in consideration of the previous chart, is ominous in terms of fatal change. Mars, Saturn, and the Sun are again angular, the Moon has now separated from the square of Jupiter, and applies to sextile the Sun. And the Sun still applies to Saturn by a true square.

We could consider this as we might a journey: the 1st house is the point of departure; the 10th the outward journey; the 7th as the destination; and the 4th as the return journey. Usually, we would look to see where the malefics are placed to find any problems. Mars and the South Node are in the 10th house, and Saturn is in the 4th, in fact, it is intercepted in the 4th. The chart confirms that the outward journey is dangerous; notice, too, that Venus and Mars are in aspect again here, and Venus disposits Mars. Pleasure is at the root of this murder. That Saturn is intercepted in the 4th argues for the hidden nature of her grave. It also suggests that as the murder took place somewhere between the bus stop and the next stage of the bus's route, Saturn indicates that the murderer returned to the terminus. The transporting Moon is in the 5th of pleasure in the last degree of Sagittarius it brings the light of that previous bad decision made by Emma in full force to Emma.

Before moving on to the last chart in this series, the details that have emerged since Emma's disappearance should be inserted. The driver of the bus, who was the usual driver of that route and so probably known slightly to Emma, was on bail awaiting a court appearance for the rape of his thirteen- -year-old babysitter. He received a custodial sentence of eighteen months for this offence, but by then Emma was missing. In 1992, it came to light through his family that he had confessed the murder of Emma to his father sometime after the event. He was questioned eventually but never charged. He died in 2006, and in 2014 the authorities made an unprecedented statement that he should have been investigated and charged. He made no further admissions and, even as he was dying, he did not reveal what he had done with Emma's body.

Reported missing
23 February 1957, 11.59 pm GMT
Coordinates as above

Having related the story, examining yet another chart might seem redundant. It seemed to me that I might be able to offer you another perspective that you will not find in any book; it is just my opinion. The chart has changed substantially and yet it is the same day with the same question: what has happened to Emma? Mars of rape and murder is still detrimented but now in the 7th house of the attacker. Venus disposits it and the Part of Death at about 13° Taurus. Venus is in the 4th of the grave as is the Sun, which was Emma's significator in the previous two figures. We can continue to accept the Sun for her and here she is in trine to the Ascendant, home. The Moon applies to sextile the Sun, surely this must mean that she will be found, but sixty-five years after her disappearance there is still no sign of her. The police made concentrated searches in 2017 but to no avail.

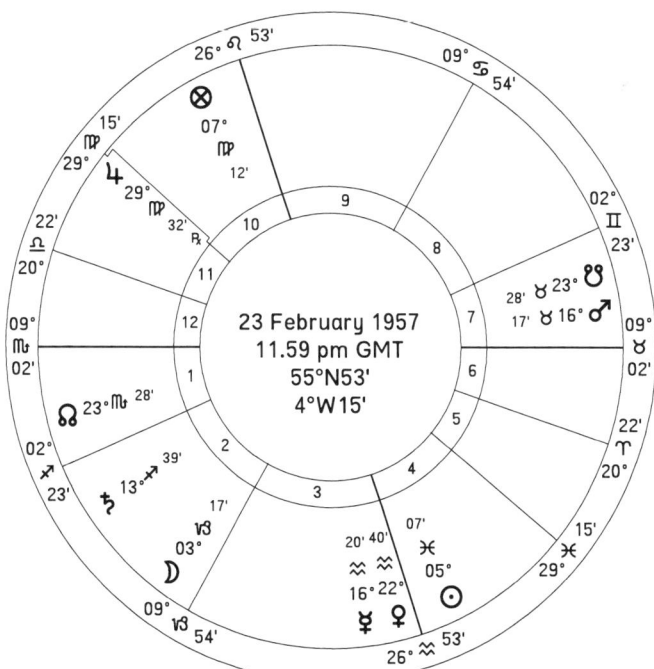

Figure 1.3
Emma: Reported missing.

Boy and Girl Missing

Last seen
31 March 1970, 5.30 pm BST
51°N40', 00°W05'

The children, aged 11 and 12 years, were reported missing by their parents when they had not returned home after going out to play together at about 4.30 pm BST. The last confirmed sighting of the two was at about 5.30 pm BST as they walked across a field. The report was made by both parents at about 8 pm at Ponders End police station. Their bodies were not discovered for nearly three months being found on 17 June 1970 in woodland.

When looking at the earlier time, we are told that they were walking across a field, so we must look at the dynamics of the event chart: they are alive and moving and we should be able to see that.

The children are signified by Mercury ruler of the double-bodied Ascendant; in Aries indicates energy and action and Mercury is an apt significator for a child. However, Mercury is in the 8th house of death, and if we can rely on the reported sighting, they are already in danger at this point. Mercury is barely in an application to conjunct Venus. Whilst it might seem odd, and I shall explain, Venus might be connected with their killer.

I suggest Venus, the lesser benefic, because of its mutual reception with Mars and because of the association with sex that both planets have particularly when working together. Mars disposits both Mercury and Venus, it is in control and is the strongest planet in this chart, and I also suggest that he persuaded them to go with him perhaps so that he might show them something of interest to children. In fact, he had picked them up in his car, given them al-

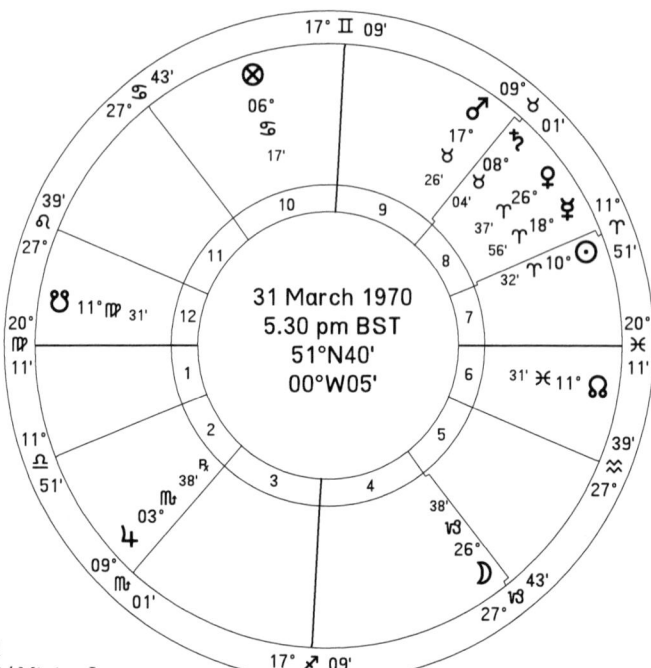

Figure 2.1
Boy and Girl Missing: Last seen.

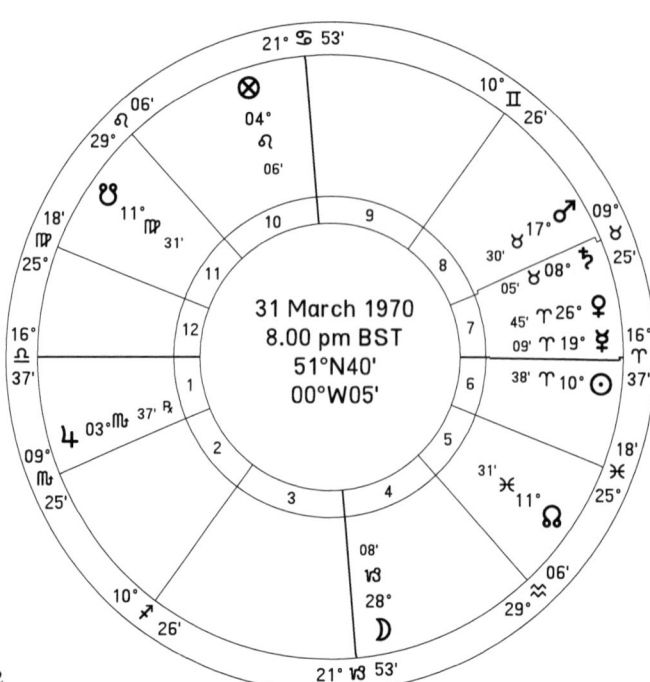

Figure 2.2
Boy and Girl Missing: Reported missing.

cohol and cannabis, and driven to the copse where he had built a 'hide' (what children used to call a 'camp'). I think that Venus's involvement here is clear.

It is quite often possible to make use of the Part of Death in ascertaining the cause of death by way of its dispositor, at least that is what I have often found in working with these charts. Here it is in Cancer disposited by the detrimented Moon in Capricorn. We might take its position at the 5th cusp as significant of pleasure and its dispositor Saturn as significant of suffocation. With both Mars and Saturn in conjunction being disposited by Venus, already suspected of involvement, we might judge beatings and suffocation (usually strangulation) as the causes of death for the purposes of sexual pleasure. Always of note in cases such as these is any connection with the two malefics whether accidental significators or not. We will see this in many of the cases to come.

In case you are wondering why I have not mentioned the ruler of the 7th house as the attacker, it is merely because the arguments are already clear without that. However, Jupiter is disposited by Mars again and is retrograde – this is not the first time he has committed such an act and may not be the last. Pisces is not a very robust sign and Jupiter is peregrine, both watery, so we might consider the attacker to be homeless or to have no fixed abode. We may assume that the opposition to peregrine Saturn exacerbates this. Saturn is also significant of imprisonment and whilst this is true of the children, it may also have been true of the attacker in that he has been in prison for some offence. Jupiter is conjunct the 3rd cusp which suggests that he is of the local area.

Reported missing
31 March 1970, 8.00 pm BST
Coordinates as above

The reported missing chart is an inception because calling the police was a conscious act, thus we might look to the 5th house for the children of the reporters (in the next case I will show you how the 1st house might also play a part). Saturn is an unusual significator for a child so attention must be given to the reason that it has arisen. Saturn is at the cusp of the 8th within 5° of it, thus counted as if in the 8th, with Mars therein and that malicious conjunction still in play. The Moon is detrimented in the 4th of the grave and I suggest that the children were already dead at this point.

The police had searched the area and had missed the hide in the corpse.

By the time that they were found decomposition was advanced and because of this at the inquest the coroner recorded an open verdict. Although the police and parents were convinced that this was clearly a case of abduction and murder, no more resources were allocated and the case was left to go 'cold'.

It was in 1996 that a convicted paedophile, already in prison for life on that account, contacted police saying that he had information regarding these murders. Two years later he said that he wanted to confess to the murders. In 2000, he pleaded guilty in court to the murders and was given two further life sentences to run concurrently with the existing one. Ultimately, he spent over 40 years in prison and died there in 2015.

His record of sexual offences began when he was fifteen years of age and by 1970 he had a long criminal record, the most serious being child sex offences and murder. He had been out of prison for similar offences for less than a month when he had killed these children. Eleven days later he was arrested for abducting and sexually abusing an eleven-year-old boy. He had happened across the two children as he was returning home from a job interview at a nearby factory. As a known sex offender who lived locally, police had interviewed him but his alibi seemed to be supported by witnesses.

World's End Murders

I have named this case because its end many years later was something of a triumph for the families bearing in mind the torment of their grief. It is also a triumph for modern forensic science and the persistence of the police. It was a remarkable case in many ways.

Christine and Helen, aged seventeen years, were out enjoying themselves for the evening. They were last seen leaving the World's End public house at closing time, about 11 pm BST. A sign of long ascension rises so an exact time is not as important as it might otherwise have been. Closing time might have been exactly at 11 pm, or a little later, or the young women may have left at 'last orders' about ten minutes earlier. It would make little difference to the chart.

The bodies of both young women were found the next day nearly ten kilometres (six miles) apart. Among other things, both had been beaten, raped, and strangled. No-one was ever charged with these murders, although there was some evidence that they had been talking to two men in the pub. The case was reopened in 1997 largely based on improvements in DNA profiling and forensic science generally; there was no match found. In 2003, further efforts were made to find a match to the unknown DNA sample and there were 200 partial matches. In the following year, a man was questioned and further swabs were taken. A few months later, Angus Robertson Sinclair was arrested and charged with the murders.

He was tried in 2007 for the murders committed with his then-deceased brother-in-law. Because the evidence was circumstantial and force could not be proved, Sinclair was acquitted; he had blamed his brother-in-law for the murders and claimed that sex was consensual. It was then revealed that he was a convicted murderer and a serial sex offender, and was serving two life sentences in this regard, having already completed one sentence for murder. One of these, a murder in 1978, was successfully tried on the basis of new DNA evidence. The 2007 acquittal caused uproar and an intense debate among the judiciary. However, in 2011 it became law that a previously tried and acquitted accused could be tried again in certain circumstances.

In 2012, the police were instructed to reopen the case of the murders of Christine and Helen and in 2014 the new trial of Sinclair began. He was found guilty of the murders and was sentenced to a minimum term of 37 years, that is, it had been 37 years since the murders; he was given a year in prison for every one of those years since he had murdered the two young women. He died in prison in 2019 aged 73 years.

Last seen
15 October 1977, 11.00 pm BST
55°N57', 3°W13'

The chart is clear and descriptive so it can be dealt with swiftly; the interest here is the length of time before the murderer was charged and found guilty.

Christine and Helen are signified by the Moon is Sagittarius having a good time in the 5th house. They have recently separated from a sextile of a fallen Venus in the 4th. One way of looking at this is that one or both young women had been given a warning before leaving home about getting drunk and about men by their parents. Notice that Mars rules the 5th and is rising in the 1st. Remember my suggestion about the Venus and Mars joint significations generally signifying sexual activity. Although both are not particular significators, Venus is angular and the Moon, the young women, separates from it. The Part of Death at 25°45' Cancer is tightly conjunct Mars indicating the motive of rape. Mars angular is significant of rape and murder without other arguments.

Saturn rules the entire southern quarter of the chart, Saturn also being significant of the attacker or attackers (in this case the latter). Sinclair's method of killing his victims usually involved strangulation, which is, of course, notably symbolic of control and silencing.

The Moon is void of course so the young women's journey will end nowhere. I say this because the Moon is mobile and changeable and when it arises as particularly significant as here, transport should be considered. One of the men had owned a camper van that had probably been used in the murders, but had been destroyed before the police could examine it. Venus, ruler of the intercepted 4th house of the deposition site, is applying to square Jupiter in signs of long ascension indicating that it was not very long before their bodies were discovered and the authorities began their work. Although exalted, Jupiter can do very little from its position in the cadent and unfortunate 12th house. However, as a weighty, superior planet, slow moving perhaps, but intent to complete its task.

Saturn, ruler of the 7th, is in the 3rd house, again indicative of someone from the local area. Stretching the signification a little, it is also the house of the brother-in-law, the Sun. Both Saturn and the Sun are in a strong mixed reception and in sextile showing them working together. In fairness, this is a retrospective realization; it does not seem likely that identifying the radical 3rd house with the brother-in-law could have been predicted without some knowledge or suspicion.

As a suggestion for further investigation, Saturn appears to be particularly involved in the charts where there is a long delay before the culprit is discovered and charged. There is little left to be said without going into unnecessary detail, except perhaps this ...

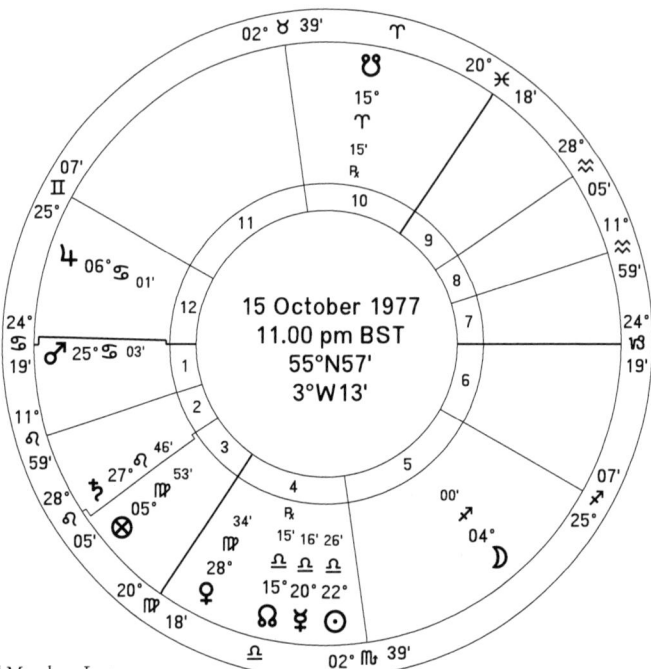

Figure 3.1
World's End Murders: Last seen.

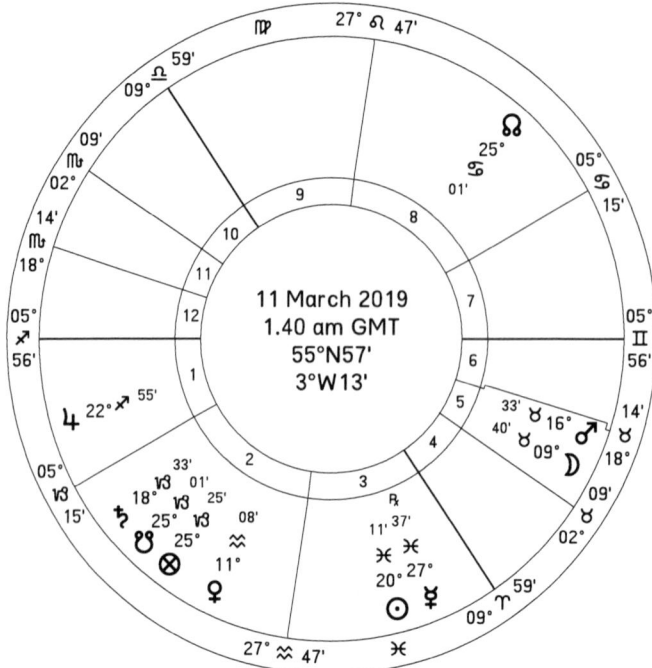

Figure 3.2
World's End Murders: Last seen (murderer).

Last seen (murderer)
11 March 2019, 1.40 am GMT
55°N53', 4°W15'

Sinclair had been in prison for most of his adult life and some may think that an easy option considering the multiplicity and awfulness of his crimes. However, the sentencing judge in 2014 had recognized a need for an acknowledgement in symbolic terms of the stolen lives of Christine and Helen by jailing him for the same 37 years since their murders. We might recall this when looking at the chart which records the last time he was seen alive. He was in the prison hospital and this was the last time nursing staff saw him alive; two hours later he was dead. He had suffered multiple strokes and heart attacks, he was incontinent and bed bound needing twenty-four-hour care. Perhaps we might take from this that his health was attacked many times for each of his victims, and that being completely helpless gave him some sense of the fear he inflicted on these young women and the others he tormented.

Look at the Ascendant, almost 6° Sagittarius rises; compare it to the young women's significator in the previous chart.

Two Girls Missing

Two girls aged nine years did not return home and were reported missing by their families at 8.30 pm BST on 9 October 1986. As part of the investigation, a report was made of a last sighting at 6.20 pm in the local area by someone who knew the girls and who had spoken to them. We might want to extend our examination into other notable times such as the time the parents last saw them which was at about 5.30 pm, but in my view two charts are enough.

Reported missing
9 October 1986, 8.30 pm BST
50°N50', 00°W08'

In this chart it makes no difference whether we take the 1st or the 5th for the children since both have Mercury as ruler and both are double-bodied signs. It is intercepted in the unfortunate 6th disposited by Mars of murder. This interception should be noted, although not found in the sources as far as I know, I think about this in the same way as Lilly describes Libra as 'one Chamber within another'.[2] Interception for me has the sense of enclosure.

The Moon is detrimented in Capricorn and it is placed on the 8th cusp. We might consider these moist signs, Cancer and Scorpio, as moist places, or giving some clue to the whereabouts of the girls (they were found a little north of their homes). The Part of Death is unfortunate in the 6th house, it is disposited by Jupiter in Pisces, again emphasizing water, but more importantly almost exactly conjunct Saturn of suffocation. Jupiter is also ruler of

---

2. William Lilly, *Christian Astrology* (London, 1985 facsimile reprint), p. 96.

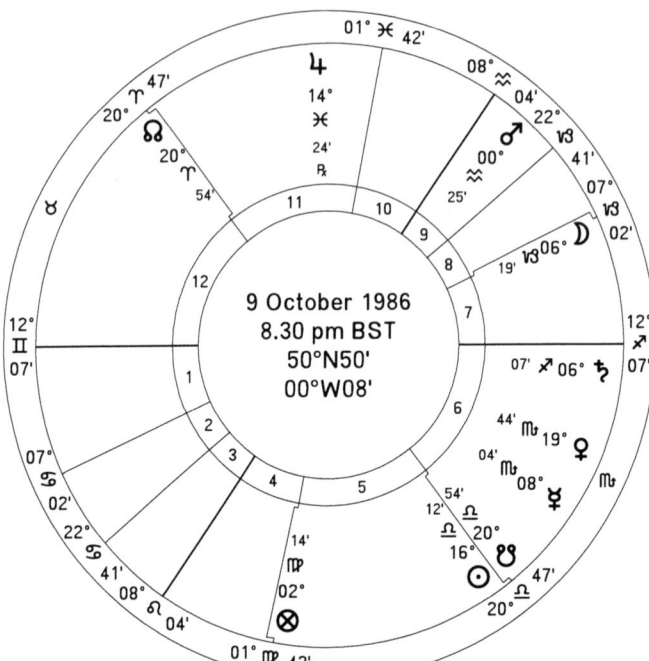

Figure 4.1
Two Girl's Missing: Reported missing.

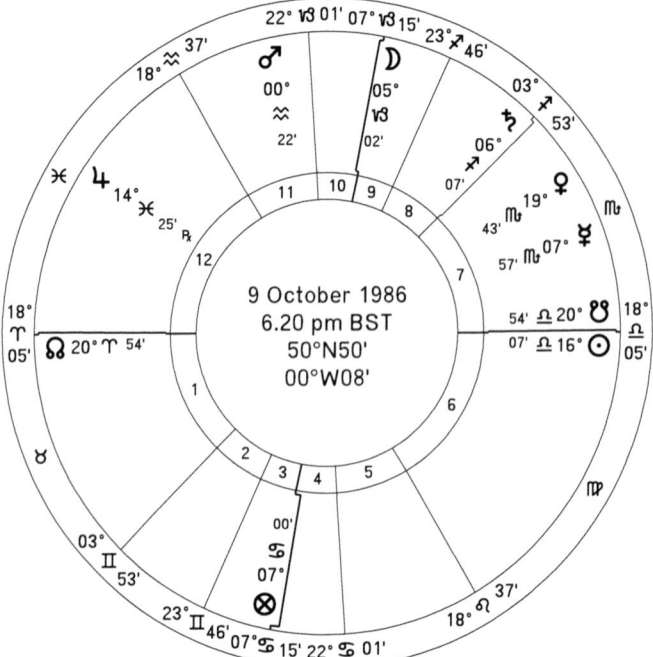

Figure 4.2
Two Girl's Missing: Last seen.

the 7th house of the fugitive and it is retrograde suggesting that this is either not the first time he has committed such an offence, or will offend in this way again, or both. This significator being retrograde is also usually a sign that the offender will return to the scene of the crime; it retrogrades to the trine of Mercury, the girls.

Remember that this is the reported missing chart, so we must consider what has happened to the girls and we therefore look to Mercury's separations. It had been in a square with Mars, and that separation is complete. It is an indication that they have been murdered. The Moon is inactive too as it separates from being void of course and has yet to complete its application to sextile Mercury. Mercury's past square with Mars indicates that something obviously unpleasant had happened, supported by the Moon's condition and position. Mars and the Moon are disposited by a debilitated and, therefore, malicious Saturn linking their deaths to suffocation. Furthermore, Mars is in an applying sextile to Saturn raising the level of malice and violence.

Last seen
9 October 1986, 6.20 pm BST
Coordinates as above

In the last seen event chart the girls are alive and well. Here they are signified by Mars, which seems somewhat odd for young girls, but even if we ignore that and use the 7th house, Venus is disposited by Mars. Mars is in a happy place in the chart but its change of sign from Capricorn where it was exalted suggests that they have moved just outside of their usual 'territory' and into a place of weakness. Where children are concerned particularly, their place of safety is where their parents are, or their home. The detrimented Moon is in the very public 10th house, actually closely conjunct the MC.

As with the previous chart, Saturn is in underlying control through its dispositorships, thus the two malefics are prominent and in aspect which is always a worrying feature. Mars applies to sextile Saturn underlining my previous remarks. Now look at what happens: Saturn is in the 8th house, it rules the 11th and Mars is in the 11th. We should also note that Saturn rules the 12th – a friend who is not a friend at all; it could not be clearer. Furthermore, we should consider that Saturn has dignity in the 7th by exaltation so it is also a known enemy. This was explained many years later as mentioned below.

In the reported missing chart, Mercury, the girls, separates from Mars; Mars has happened to them. In the last seen chart, Mars, the girls, applies to Saturn; Saturn will happen to them. The malevolent intervention of Mars and Saturn in both charts is ominous boding ill for the girls.

Their bodies were found the next day in what children would call a 'camp' or 'den' in the trees of Wild Park. They had been sexually assaulted and strangled, although later it was found that at least one of the girls had been beaten. This is exactly what could be expected from the presence of Mars and Saturn. As might also be adduced from the astrology, they died very soon after the last sighting.

A suspect was arrested later in the month, he had been present as part of the search for the girls and had 'discovered' the site. It was later assumed that he had attempted to contaminate the scene so that any traces of him could be justified in that way. In 1987, he was acquitted of the rape and murder of the two girls. Apart from the forensic evidence being called into question, it was suggested that the girls had been seen at 6.30 pm when the accused had been seen leaving the park not going to it. His defence was assisted when his girlfriend at the time recanted her evidence that a sweatshirt found near the site of the murders and holding traces of one of the girls was his. He was known to the girls and had called at one of the girls' houses earlier in the day. Apparently, the girl insulted his girlfriend making him very angry. However, in 1990, he was convicted of a similar offence against a seven-year-old girl who had survived and for which he received a sentence of at least fourteen years.

In 2005, the double jeopardy law was changed which meant that a suspect could be tried a second time for a crime if there was substantial new evidence, but this could be done only once. In 2016, he was arrested again on the previous charges. In 2017, the previous acquittals were made void leaving the way open to try him again. He appeared at the Old Bailey in 2018 to answer for the former charges. He was ultimately found guilty and given a life sentence recommended to be no less than thirty-six years. His former girlfriend, who had given him an alibi in 1987, was found guilty in 2021 of perjury and perverting the course of justice. She was sentenced to six years in prison.

As with the other cases that have been resolved after many years, a comparison with the charts of the final arrest, charge, or conviction would be very useful.

WK and CP

The inclusion of these two cases is because of the strangeness of them and, again, because of the length of time between committing these offences and the murderer being caught. The conclusion of these cases could only be described as bizarre.

WK last seen
22 June 1987, 11.00 pm BST
51°N08', 00°E16'

WK's boyfriend dropped her off at her home just after 11 pm BST after an evening out. She was 25 years old. After staff at her place of work told her boyfriend the next day that she had not arrived, he went to her flat and found her dead; she had been beaten, strangled, and sexually assaulted post mortem.

A sign of short ascension rises in early degrees; at 11.05 pm the Ascendant has moved on just over 4° and all the planets maintain their house positions. If the chart is advanced by ten minutes, Venus moves back into the 4th house giving some angularity, otherwise there is none, which is unusual. Saturn would remain ruler of the Ascendant even if the time were earlier and this should come as no surprise given the manner of her death. Saturn is in the 11th of a safe haven and the Moon is exalted in the 3rd. It has been reported that the killer had broken in and was waiting for her inside her flat, but Saturn is retrograde and only just inside the 11th house. Is it possible that he knocked at the door as soon as she arrived home, and that retrograde motion shows her going back to the door to her flat? The Moon separates from a sextile with Mars and is void of course; I think the symbolism here is obvious and needs

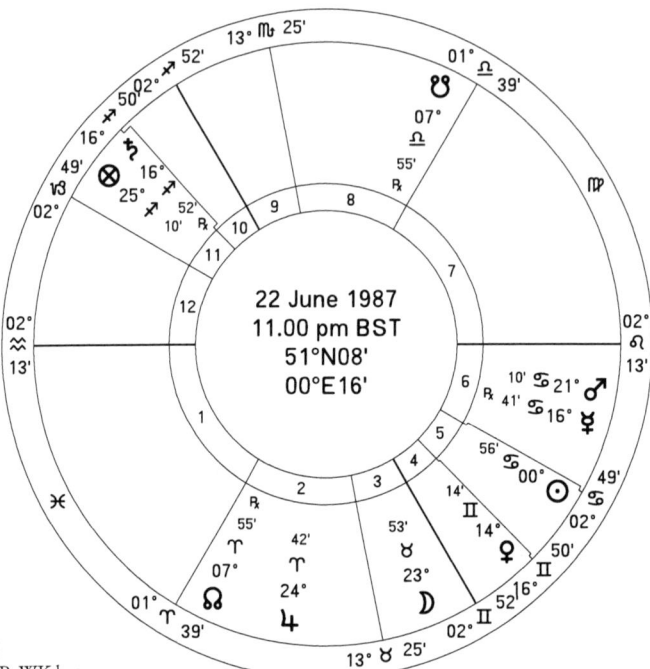

Figure 5.1
WK and CP: WK last seen.

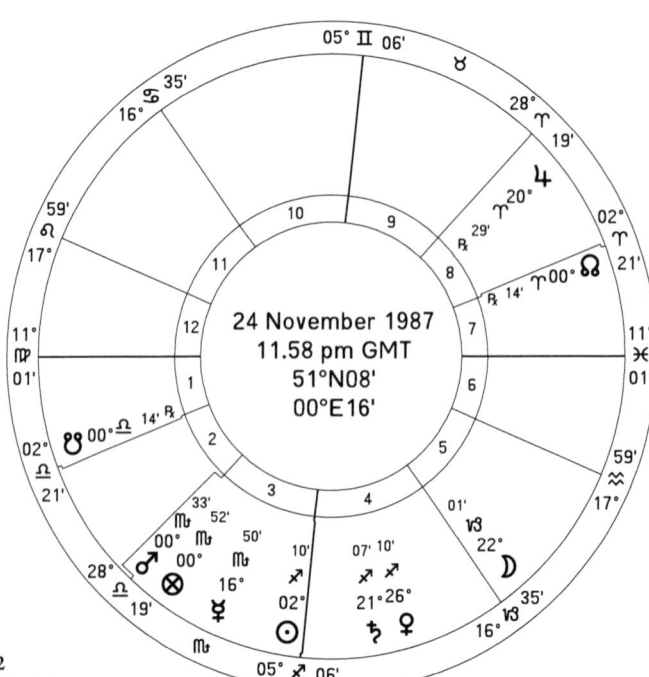

Figure 5.2
WK and CP: CP last seen.

no further elucidation. The Part of Death at 24°38' Aries adds weight to the argument that rape was the motive and Venus is mutually separating from the opposition of Saturn, linking Venus and Mars again in this context. Venus is ruler of the 8th house of death in the 5th of pleasure and even if the time is different and Venus is in the 4th its natural rulership of pleasure maintains. The connection of Venus with the 8th house and Saturn should be kept in mind for a little later.

Finding arguments for capture can be tricky, but here Mars, as the murderer, is applying to square Jupiter ruler of the 10th house of authority. But the distance between them cannot equate to the 32 years it took to conclude these cases.

CP last seen
24 November 1987, 11.58 pm GMT
Coordinates as above

CP, aged 20 years, was dropped off at her flat by a taxi at about this time five months later in the same area. She was reported missing the next day, again because she had failed to turn up for work. Her body was found three weeks later; she had been attacked similarly to WK. It appears that she was abducted from outside of her flat.

A sign of long ascension rises so inaccuracy of time will make little difference if it is not too great. Sun, Saturn, and Venus are angular in the 4th, although the latter two are some distance from the cusp. Strictly, we should take Mercury for CP, and we shall eventually, but I am interested in the position of the Sun just before the cusp of the 4th; does this indicate CP at her door? Should we not then look at Jupiter, the Sun's dispositor, as her abductor, especially as it rules the 7th house? Jupiter is retrograde in the 8th of death: he has done this before. Jupiter is in a close trine with Saturn and disposits Saturn; Saturn is strongly implied in the manner of death. Jupiter also disposits the Part of Death at 1°27' Pisces, but how could Jupiter provide a motive? Jupiter is unfortunate: it is retrograde, in the unfortunate 8th, in aspect to malefic Saturn, and very poorly dignified. An unfortunate Jupiter is excessive, not quite as much as a natural malefic is, but enough and when placed in choleric Aries we have a strong argument for a frenzied attack. With Saturn's involvement we might also want to consider obsession as a driving force. The detrimented Moon in the 5th of pleasure separates from the square with Jupiter (in signs of short ascension) and applies to a sextile of Mars, ruler of the 8th, in viperous Scorpio.

Recalling the mobility of the Moon with Mars in the 3rd house of short distance travel and knowing that CP was not at home, it would be reasonable to conclude that she was carried away in a vehicle. There is some verification of that because Mercury, ruler of the Ascendant, is intercepted in the 3rd, imprisoned and dominated by Mars. Since Mars rules the 8th house, it is possible that she was already dead at this point.

DF was arrested in December 2020 based on a new investigation focusing on improved DNA profiling. Police attended his home address and arrested him on suspicion of killing WK and CP. During the search of those premises that followed his arrest, hard drives, floppy discs, DVDs, and memory cards were discovered. Millions of images were found of DF sexually abusing corpses in the mortuary of the hospital where he worked as an electrician. These images ranged between 2008 and 2020, just prior to his arrest, and are of his abuse of a few men, a few children, but mostly women. Since he had labelled some of these images with names, relatives were contacted, but in some cases this was impossible. The full details of these abuses are too shocking to list here, but suffice it to say that he pleaded guilty to fifty-one offences, including forty-four relating to seventy-eight unidentified victims. He also eventually pleaded guilty to murdering WK and CP. He was given a whole life sentence meaning that he will never be released.

We might recall the Venus-Saturn configurations in both charts and perhaps consider them as significant of necrophilia.

Murdered Family

This case was one that I judged at the time and my findings were passed on to the police responsible for the investigation. It has become a rather well known case with the convictions being challenged unofficially.

Reported to police
13 July 1994, 2.01 am PDT
47°N37', 122°W12'

Two young men, friends on holiday from college, arrived at the home of the parents of one of them after a night out. What I did not know at the time was that the son's friend had been staying at the house and was there when the bodies were found and indeed, had made the call to the police. They discovered the parents and the sister who had been bludgeoned apparently with a baseball bat, the parents were dead, the sister still alive but died the next day. The mother was found downstairs just inside the garage door; the father and daughter were in separate rooms upstairs.

Having now read the many reports that are available on the internet which were not at the time, it is clear that the two young men had solid alibis for the time between leaving the house at about 8.30 pm PDT and arriving home and making the call to the police. In fact, the alibis were so solid that the police suspected that they had been carefully constructed to avoid suspicion. If so, and the young men were the killers, then presumably the killings took place before they left the house, there being little time after the arrived home.

However, I had none of this information at the time and the next I heard was that they had left the country and that the police had not had enough evidence against them. Eventually, extradition proceedings began and they were returned to America in 2001 on the understanding that they would not be executed if found guilty.

The chart is timed for the call made to the police where very late degrees of Taurus rise; a marker of death. Mars of murder is in the 1st house and, again, there is the malice of Saturn in a mutually applying square in signs of short ascension. Mutual application implies suddenness, which, in this context, might suggest impulsiveness. Mars rules the 7th of known enemies and the 12th of secret enemies, those we think of as our friends, and which is amplified by Saturn being in the 11th of friendship and assistance.

The 1st is ruled by Venus and describes the victims, Virgo showing more than one. It is in the 5th of children of the 1st, so the brother and sister. The Sun of life rules the 5th and it might be said that with the Moon applying to it by sextile, the sister's brief survival is described. The Part of Death is at about 24° Gemini disposited by Mercury which is in a sextile with Venus in signs of long ascension which makes this aspect more like a square introducing tension into this relationship. Mercury rules the intercepted 5th house and disposes of Venus and the Moon, as well as Mars itself. Its mutual reception with the Moon and the mixed reception with Mars in an Air sign hint at harsh words, a row perhaps. Mercury and the Part of Death are in the 2nd house leading to an indication of a row about money. Mercury is also the natural ruler of young men in particular. Mars as the murderer in the 1st indicates that the murderer was at the scene when they were found.

It was for all of these reasons that I suggested that the son was responsible for these deaths. As I mentioned previously, I did not know that the friend had been there but taking Mars as the murderer and the connection with Saturn in the 11th and ruling the 11th probably gives a reasonable description; as does the double-bodied sign in which Mars is placed. However, that does not explain Saturn's interception, since this often provides a description of enclosure in some form, perhaps some kind of coercion was used to gain the friend's cooperation. I have not found anything like that in the subsequent reports but it is a reasonable assumption.

There had been three large insurance policies, one that paid out immediately, this and the value of the house they had lived in was taken as evidence of motive. In 2004, the young men were found guilty of murder and given three life sentences each. There are unofficial attempts to overturn these sentences calling the evidence into question. But that was not my remit. However, I had judged that because Saturn's involvement and ruling the 10th that it would take a long time for this case to be finally resolved.

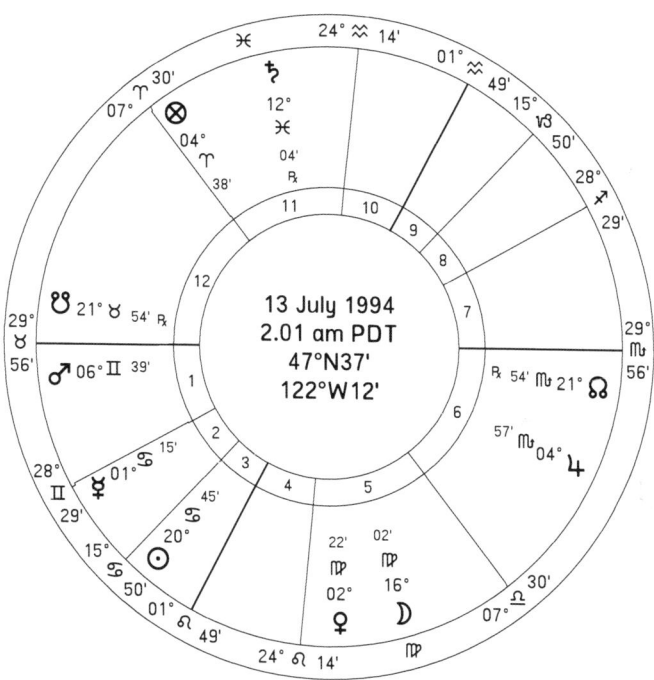

Figure 6.1
Murdered Family: Reported to police.

Lise

Lise was eighteen years old and had been celebrating Christmas with friends at a disco. They left the disco at 2 am GMT (recorded on CCTV) and went to get something to eat, after which, and turning down two offers of a lift home, Lise started out on the ten-minute walk to her home. This was the last time anyone saw her alive. This time is approximate, but with a sign of long ascension rising, the twenty-minutes' difference from the CCTV time will not make a great deal of difference.

Last seen
25 December 1995, 2.20 am GMT
51°N27', 2°W35'

The first thing I noticed was that Venus and Mars ruled the Ascendant and Descendant. Recalling other cases where, in the right context, their appearance can describe crimes of sexual assault. The next point of early interest is the angularity; Lise's significator, Venus, is in the 4th with the Moon, both disposited by Saturn, and both void of course. This house and Saturn are associated with delay and detention (as well as the grave). So, as a last-seen time and with no further information, it would be reasonable to assume that something had happened to Lise to delay her return home, or that she had been detained. Especially having both of her significators void of course, the suggestion is that she will not reach her intended destination at all.

Mars and Saturn are yet again co-operating, so this first opinion could be extended to include danger and threat. They are exactly sextile, Mars being exalted in Capricorn; I always consider the characteristic of arrogance in connection with exaltation – someone who will not take 'no' for an answer. Mars

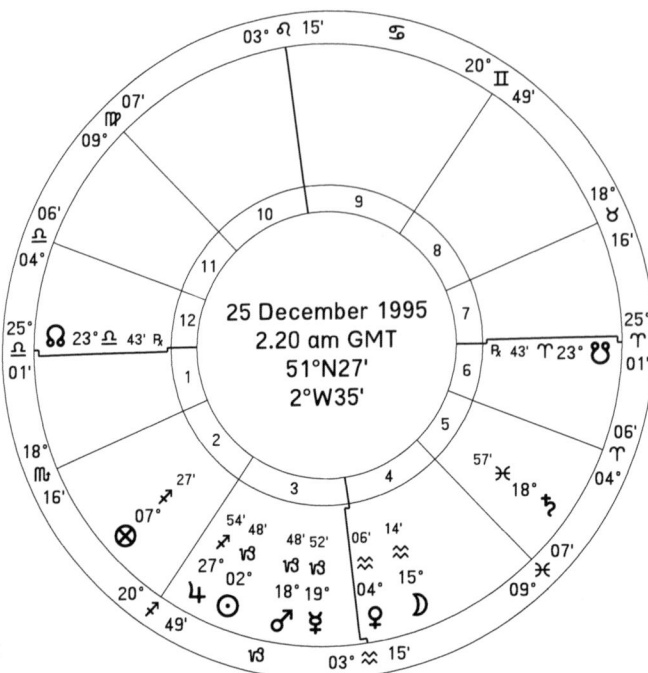

Figure 7.1
Lise: Last seen.

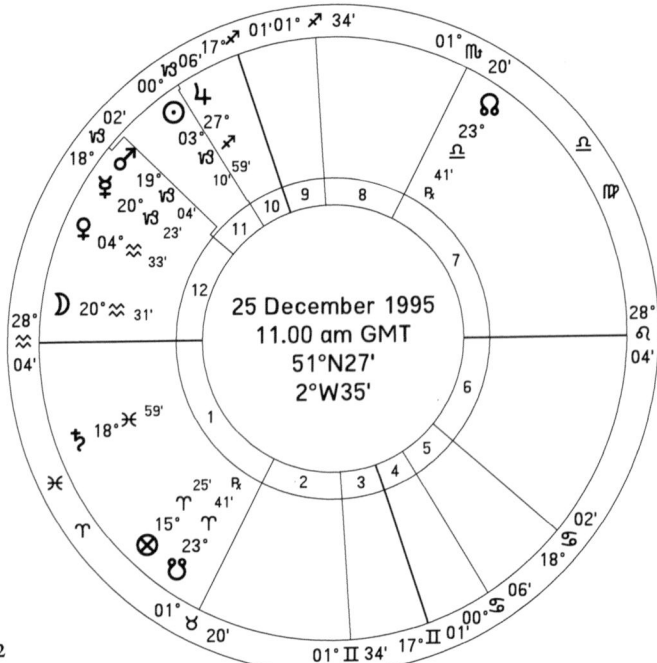

Figure 7.2
Lise: Reported missing.

also rules the 7th house of the attacker, if one is suspected. Is there enough evidence here to judge that harm has come to Lise? Each of these configurations is a concern: the Venus-Mars implications certainly raise suspicions; the Mars-Saturn involvement adds weight to those suspicions. One more indication perhaps leads to the conclusion of harm – the Part of Death at 22° Gemini disposited by Mercury which is in the 3rd house of the local area and is disposited by Saturn of smothering, or strangulation. I want to add a small, personal note here: frequently, in cases where sexual abuse is involved, strangulation is a common method of 'silencing' the victim actually and symbolically. That is not to say, of course, that death generally is not the final 'silencer'. But silencing the victim can be the instinctive response where the victim's voice is the primary issue in the violence. Suffocation is a demonstration of power over the victim, but, once physically overpowered, it also robs her of her last chance of defence - her voice.

Reported missing
25 December 1995, 11.00 am GMT
Coordinates as above

Lise's parents realised the next morning, Christmas morning, that she had not returned home. After ringing all her friends without success, they rang the police.

The 4th house of the previous chart rises with very late degrees; again a sign of death. There is a double interception in the 1st house, Pisces and Aries being wholly enclosed there. Saturn is in the 1st, the Moon is in the 12th house of sorrow disposited by Saturn. Of course Mars and Saturn are still in aspect. The Part of Death at 29°48' Scorpio enlarges that connection because Mars is the dispositor of it in exalted and in the 12th house.

There is little point in arguing about which planet symbolizes Lise and which her parents. We could say that Saturn is for the parents, worried and distraught, and the Moon, Lise, as ruler of the 5th house, or we could simply allow the chart to 'speak'. The only angularity is Saturn of death in sextile to Mars of murder and ruler of the 8th of death.

The late degrees mentioned twice in this chart might also be descriptive of where she was found. Lise's body was found by two boys on 17 February 1996 in a disused quarry. She had been left on a ledge high up and covered with branches. Late degrees emphasize edges, thresholds, and similar points of change, and, although I would not put too much weight on it, Aquarius is associated specifically with quarries. The reason for my hesitancy is that locations in this context are rarely that clear and straightforward.

A huge DNA sweep of the local male population revealed nothing and it was some two years before it was realised that a man who had been identified from the CCTV footage from the nightclub had not given a DNA sample. This person was a student and had left the country on a work experience project. A test kit was sent to the police of that country and following the results of that, detectives from Britain flew out to question him.

His defence was that he had picked her up as she walked home and she had agreed to go with him. He said that they had had sex and that she had become upset and began to scream. In his attempts to stop her from screaming by putting his hand over her mouth, he had killed her. Lise had been found naked which, he said, was part of their 'sexual encounter'. It was bitterly cold in a particularly cold winter, forensic evidence had been preserved because of it. Why would she have removed all of her clothes leaving only her shoes on? At the outset, the prosecution were going to proceed with a charge of rape, but they agreed to drop that when he pleaded guilty to her murder. Perhaps there was not enough evidence to prove force; the clothing perhaps was not ripped or torn and the decomposition of the body after nearly two months in the open and being disturbed by animals may have destroyed other evidence of force. The location of the body was not easy to access being overgrown with no proper path to it; Lise had been to a disco in her party clothes and shoes presumably, would she have agreed to go with a stranger to such a place and risk spoiling her clothes?

There are no answers to these questions in the evidence but the astrology brings out the arrogance and malice of that Mars-Saturn combination. He could not simply have held his hand over her mouth, he also had to hold her down and she would have been struggling.

He received a fourteen-year sentence.

Lina

Lina was found on 25 August 1996, she had been beaten and was found partially submerged in a river near to her last sighting, she had drowned; there was no sexual assault.

This case was reopened by police in 2016 and the time of the first chart is taken from those reports rather than the contemporary reports which gave various times for this first last-seen event.

Leaves friend
24 August 1996, 11.54 pm BST
55°N59', 4°W36'

Lina, 14 years old, turned down her friend's offer to walk home with her saying that she was going to her boyfriend's house. Lina is represented by Mercury ruler of the 1st house. At this point she is in a position of strength in her own sign and house, the 5th, with the Sun of life conjunct that cusp. She had had a fun time with her friend and now she would change her location as Mercury changes its sign and moves into Libra. The Moon is in detriment just in the 8th house – we might want to reconsider this because a sign of short ascension rises and a few minutes of time can make a lot of difference to some of these cusps. Just two minutes later and the Moon is in the 7th house, but remains in conjunction with the 8th cusp.

What difference does this make to the judgement? In the 8th, the Moon is supporting Mercury's testimony of the end of life. In the 7th with a fallen Jupiter, demands more attention to the 7th house. Lina had told her friend that she was going to see her boyfriend, and he could be the 7th house. He is not

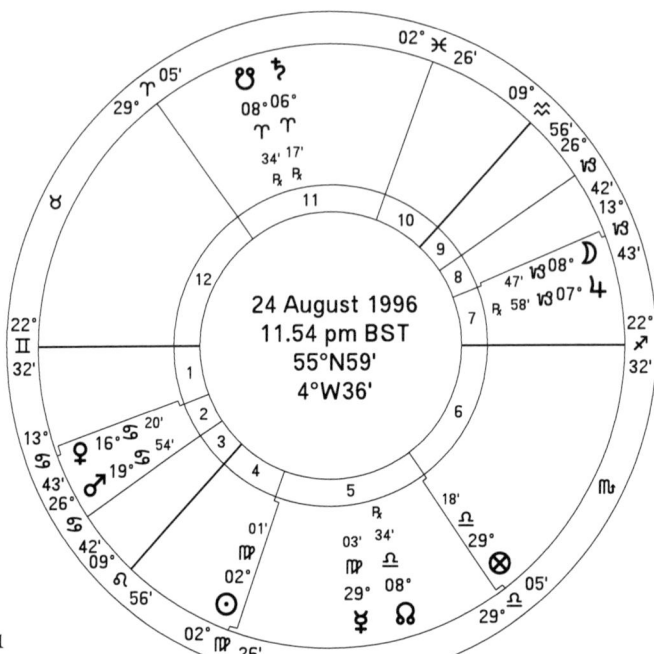

Figure 8.1
Lina: Leaves friend.

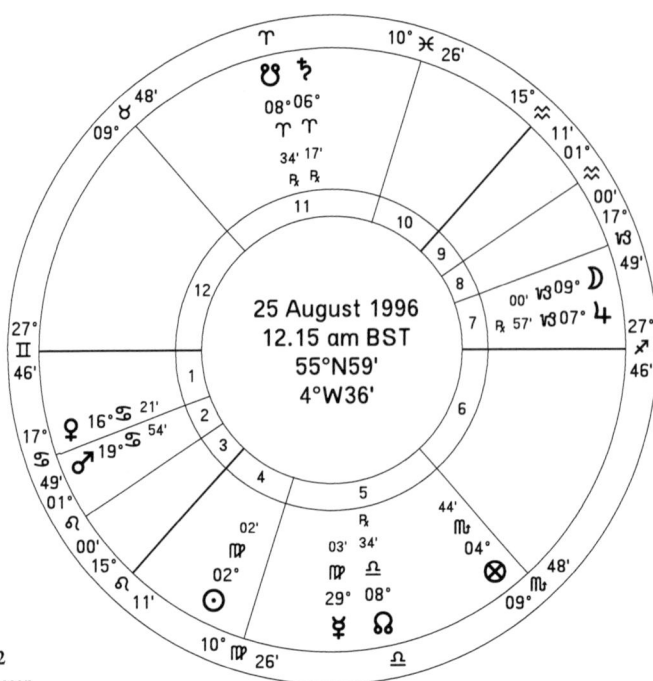

Figure 8.2
Lina: Last seen.

a person that most parents would approve of for their daughter, Jupiter is in detriment, and in a retrograde application – the worst of all applications – to an aspect with fallen Saturn. Saturn is in the 11th house of friends and is disposited by Mars in the 2nd house. I have pointed out in other cases that Mars and Saturn involvements in these contexts often indicate great nastiness and malice. Although there is no direct contact here or angularity, I would look at these dispositorships as indicating some spitefulness in the background, or behind what led up to Lina's disappearance. Also, the Part of Death at 11°13' Aries is disposited by Mars in the 2nd, emphasizing money. The Moon, too, is applying to oppose Venus in the 2nd whilst also dispositing it. This close connection between the Moon and Jupiter could indicate that he had another girlfriend.

Although the time is a little uncertain, there is clearly a problem showing in this chart for a young girl out for the evening and on her way to meet her boyfriend (I have not overlooked the time that she was out on the streets). Also noting that only Jupiter is angular – the Moon is too possibly – far from the Descendant and in fall. This definitely brings the boyfriend into the foreground, not forgetting that it also rules the 11th of friends. These arguments suggest that whomever killed Lina was not a stranger.

Last seen
25 August 1996, 12.15 am BST
Coordinates as above

A taxi driver who knew Lina spotted her walking alone near the river with a man walking along behind her (I do not think he was ever identified). This again is an approximate time with a similar chart resulting from it as would be expected.

The Sun is now in the 4th house, and Mercury, Lina, is still on home territory, but the degree of the Ascendant is now late. The Moon and Jupiter are definitely within the 7th house maintaining rulership of the 7th, 11th, and 2nd houses. Screams were heard at around this time or a little later, but there are conflicting reports about this. It seems clear that Lina was attacked soon after this chart.

There is little that can be added to the previous judgement: both charts speak of her involvement with friends and that there may have been an argument over money. It is difficult to see how this might have led to the severe attack on Lina that had led to her death.

Having reopened the case in 2016, on 25 October 2021, two men and a woman appeared in court charged with the murder of Lina; one of them was the man said to have been her boyfriend. At the time of writing, they are awaiting trial.

Vee

Vee and a friend, both seventeen years old, had been to a nightclub and at about 1 am BST had decided to walk the just over three kilometres (two miles) to their homes. They parted company at the end of Vee's road at about 2.20 am BST and that was the last time Vee was seen alive. Her parents realised that she had not returned home and reported her missing at 8.20 am on the same day.

Last seen
19 September 1999, 2.20 am BST
51°N58', 1°E20'

Leo rises and so the Sun represents Vee, and Mercury, ruler of the 11th, her friend. They are placed in the 3rd house of the local area and in different signs because they were parting ways at this point with Vee turning into her road, a very short distance from her home, and her friend continuing on. Venus in the 1st is indicative of the evening at the nightclub. Further angularity is found in Saturn and Jupiter both retrograde and intercepted in the 10th house, and both disposited by Venus.

Looking again at the Sun and Mercury in the 3rd house, this house can be considered as that of short distance travel, local travel. Although separating, the Sun remains in trine with Saturn, ruler of the 7th and 8th houses. This connects Vee with the abductor and death even though the aspect is waning. In my opinion, this echoes the fact that Saturn is intercepted, in hiding. Did he follow them in his vehicle? Was he waiting for them to separate? Did he know where Vee lived? Had he almost given up when the last chance occurred as Vee walked towards her front door? But the least that can be said for Saturn

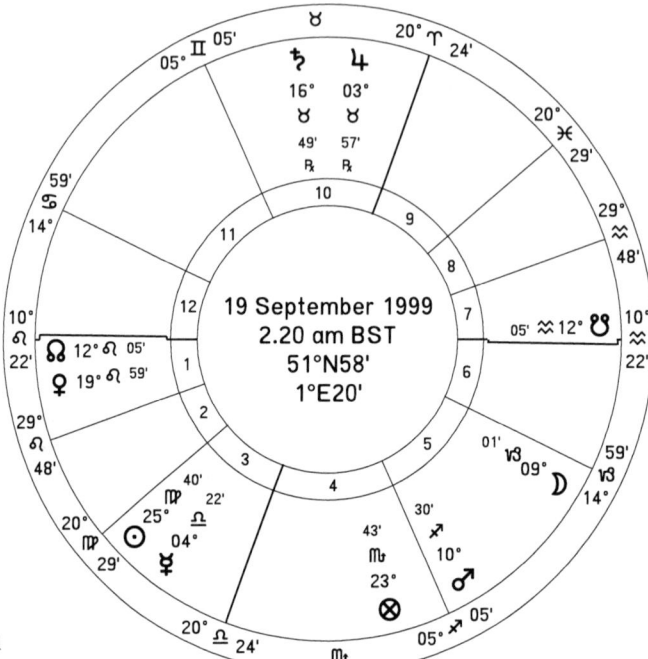

Figure 9.1
Vee: Last seen.

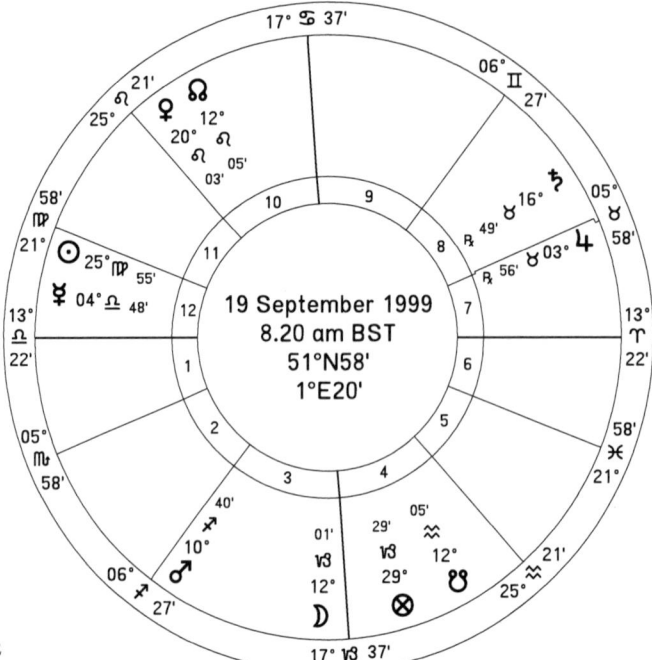

Figure 9.2
Vee: Reported missing.

in Taurus is that it is patient. Did he know that she lived in the street? He had to be very quick; she was only a few metres away from her house. Vee's friend reported that she heard two screams as she walked away but had assumed that it was someone pretending. Neighbours reported hearing a vehicle roaring away and sounding like a sports car.

It seems that he grabbed her from the street, pushed her into his vehicle and drove off at speed. It is likely that he subdued her possibly by knocking her out, although there were no reports of her being beaten. From this position of a journey, we can note the Moon because it is representative of travel, and it is the natural significator of the chart. The Moon is in detriment, unfortunate as ruler of the 12th, and mutually applying to the trine of Saturn. A journey to her death. Noticing too that the Part of Death at 7°36' Cancer is disposited by that nasty Moon. What could this have to do with a motive? There is a strong mixed reception between the Moon and Saturn and the aspect has already been noted. This is a person who simply wants to do something nasty with a warped sense of control: he can if he wants to.

Reported missing
19 September 1999, 8.20 am BST
Coordinates as above

The only angular planet is Venus again, in the 10th house this time, in public. It makes no difference to the judgement however accidental significators might be decided. If we take Venus as ruler of the 1st as Vee she is isolated and void of course, although visible. Venus rules the 8th house and has separated from the square with Saturn placed in the 8th house. We might assume the 1st for her parents making the call, and giving the 5th to Vee. Saturn is in the 8th and that decrepit Moon still mutually applies to it. There does not seem to be any point in trying to wring out more information from this chart, we have our answer already.

Her body was found in a water-filled ditch at the edge of a field some thirty-two kilometres (twenty miles) from her home. She had been strangled but had not been sexually assaulted. Perhaps this is described by the lack of involvement of Mars, and perhaps Venus.

No-one has ever been charge with Vee's murder. However, following new evidence, a man was arrested in July 2021 for this murder. Although the police will neither confirm nor deny it, it has been reported that the man arrested is a known serial killer already serving a full life sentence for a series of murders he committed in 2006. At the time of writing, he remains under investigation.

Sharon

Sharon, 9 years old, who had never walked home from school on her own was last seen by her friend as they parted at the school gates at the usual time. Sharon did not reach home.

Last seen
19 February 2008, 3.10 pm GMT
53°N42', 1°W37'

Sharon is represented by the Sun as ruler of the rising sign; it is in very early degrees of Pisces in the 8th house of death and danger. It applies to the opposition of Saturn, which is ominous. The Moon is in the 1st house and is void of course having separated from Mercury, ruler of the 11th house of friends. Mercury is in Aquarius in the 7th house and, unusually, Venus applies to its conjunction. Venus rules the 4th and the intercepted 10th houses. Mercury rules the 3rd and 11th houses; there is a strong mutual reception between it and Saturn.

The attentive reader will have noticed that I do not usually simply list all the astrology like this, and there is a reason for it. In every chart of whatever sort, any angularity must be addressed, and here the Moon and Mercury are prominently placed across the Ascendant-Descendant axis. Without considering accidental significations, the Moon and Mercury are connected with movement and transport. It would not be unreasonable to suppose that Sharon had been carried away. Clearly, the child can do nothing to help herself; the Sun's application to Saturn can only indicate imprisonment at best. The Sun is in very early degrees which suggests that her location has changed only slightly. The Part of Death at 21°21' Aquarius is disposited by Saturn of deten-

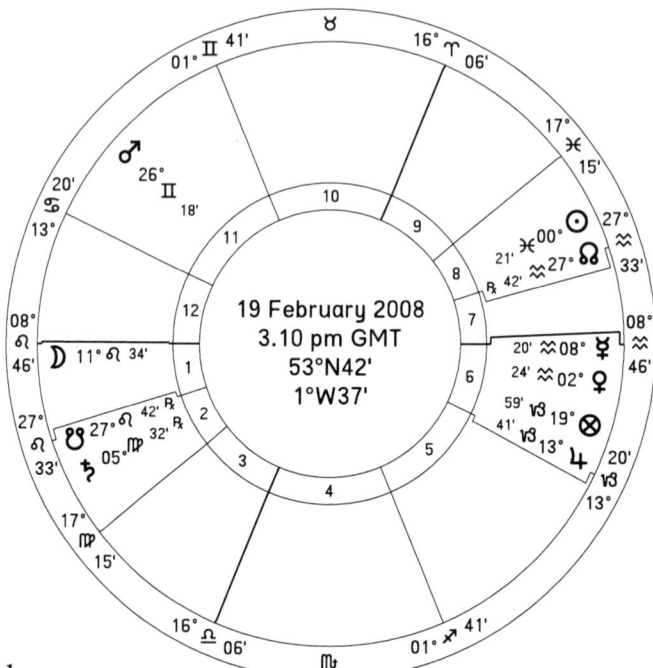

Figure 10.1
Sharon: Last seen.

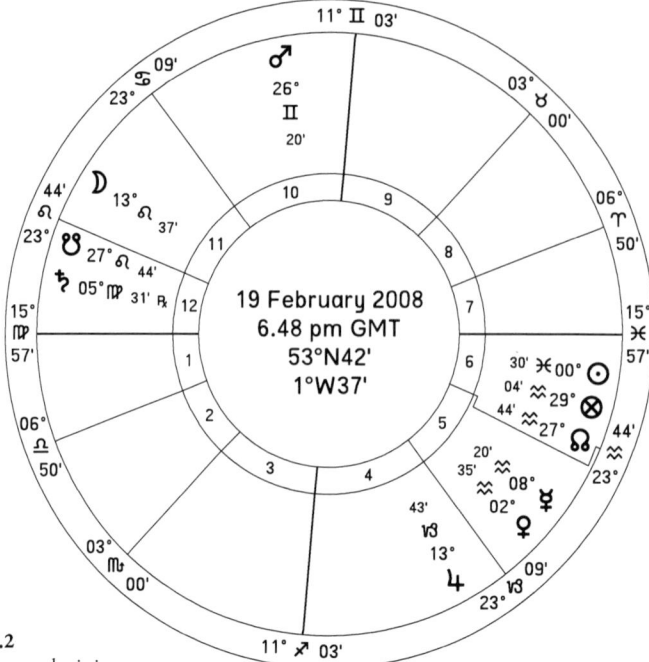

Figure 10.2
Sharon: Reported missing.

tion, death, and silence through its being disposited by Mercury. This chart seems to speak of danger and/or death.

Reported missing
19 February 2008, 6.48 pm GMT
Coordinates as above

The mother reported her as missing to the police at this time. This resulted in a massive police investigation, the mobilizing of the local community, and immense national publicity. This is clear from Mercury's being in trine to the MC. Again, whether we choose the 1st as the mother making the call with the 5th as Sharon, or the 1st as Sharon and the 10th as her mother, is unimportant. Mercury is the mother in any case, and Saturn is closely involved with Mercury (as it was in the previous chart), and the Moon is still within orbs of that opposition with Mercury.

The angularity is odd: Mars in Gemini in the 10th, and Jupiter in Capricorn in the 4th. It is difficult to find anything much to say about it, and that should not be because this is the time when the mother, so distraught that she is forced to call the police, expresses her fears. Mercury is in the 5th; is that her daughter's house? How can that be? If Mercury is Sharon and the mother, then why is it in the 5th with Venus applying to it? What are all those receptions between it and Saturn retrograde in the 12th? It did not make sense to me and neither did the last-seen chart. So I tested it against the rules for the truthfulness of a report in *Christian Astrology* (p. 192). If the Moon is void of course, as here, the report is unimportant, lies that will soon be contradicted; if the Moon opposes Mercury the news/report is false and made in order to scare people. This report is a lie.

In the afternoon of 14 March 2008, the police found Sharon alive. She had been drugged with temazepam and tied to a long rope attached to the ceiling so that she could not leave the room. When the police had knocked at the door she was made to hide in the base of a divan bed with her abductor. Someone had told the police that they had not seen their friend and drinking pal since Sharon had gone missing; he was used to seeing him everyday. On arriving at the address, a neighbour told the police that they had heard a child's footsteps above, which was the reason that they had persisted in gaining entry.

The man, whom she obviously knew, had picked up Sharon from school and he had then hidden her in his flat, taking her out to the park at night for exercise. Tests showed that Sharon had been given temazapam for some twenty months before her kidnap.

The man holding Sharon prisoner was the uncle of her mother's boyfriend. Sharon's mother and the man had planned to release Sharon, pretend to 'find' her, then claim the reward of £50,000. Both received sentences of eight years.

JH

This was a macabre case and the full, gory details will not be provided here. The first part of his body was found in a green holdall. Further parts were found in various locations on 29 March, 31 March, 7 April, and 11 April; all of his body has not been found.

As soon as the first part was found, it was clear that a murder has taken place, at least, that is a reasonable assumption. At this point, the victim had not been identified and an astrological chart is not going to provide a name and address, but we can see if the murder and murderer are described. Perhaps then adding this to further information as it is received.

1st body part found
22 March 2009, 5.00 pm GMT
51°N55', 00°E14'

Saturn rises retrograde with a double-bodied Ascendant; its ruler is in the 7th detrimented and in fall in another double-bodied sign. Mars rules the 8th house and is in the 6th again in a double-bodied sign. The Part of Death at 12°53' Scorpio is of course disposited by Mars already mentioned. Needless to say, great attention needs to be given to Mars because of the astrology and the nature of the disposal of the corpse. The Moon applies to conjunct Jupiter in the 5th and Jupiter rules the 4th of the deposition site also a double-bodied sign. Mercury separates from the opposition with Saturn, indicative of death and I shall return to this. The descriptions seem clear but how might we identify the killer?

Jupiter will also be speaking of the killer because it rules the 7th and disposits Mercury, the victim. The Moon separates from Venus and applies to Jupiter; between the two benefics should indicate safety even though Venus is detrimented and Jupiter is peregrine; a false haven. The Moon rules the 11th house of trust, Venus rules the 2nd of money, and Jupiter, as said, rules the 7th of enemies, also the 4th. Being in the 5th house does not seem to mean a lot, but it opens up a little when taken as the 11th house turned from the 7th. The idea of friendship and trust arises again.

Still, Mars has to figure strongly in this case, it has to, and yet it is in the cadent 6th not prominent at all. But why is it in the 6th? What does that have to do with anything? Questions like these usually need to be asked because signification and house placement are never random.

Cutting a fairly long story short, JH had allowed a friend and his girl-friend to stay at his flat with him, and this had been for about four months. The friendship had broken down because of various unwelcome impositions and petty thefts and a refusal to pay any rent. This had led to disputes and he had asked them to leave; he had complained about this to a friend around the time of the previous Christmas. So, we see the connection of the 11th houses, radical and turned, and the 6th house of tenants. Saturn angular opposing the victim must have some signification for his death and it appears that having been stabbed, the murderer's girlfriend put a pillow over the victim's mouth to 'stifle the noise'. The stab wounds did not kill him outright apparently, but perhaps suffocation did, although she was acquitted of murder. Once JH was dead, they used his credit cards and bank account and sold his car to spend on trivial items.

He was imprisoned for a minimum of 36 years and will not be eligible for parole until 2046. She received three years and nine months.

In case you are wondering why Saturn is retrograde in that prominent position, it transpired in court that he had dismembered four other bodies between 1995 and 1998. He would give no further information about them. So, he had done it before, often a feature of a retrograde significator and, of course, he had returned to the scene of the crime: the victim's flat.

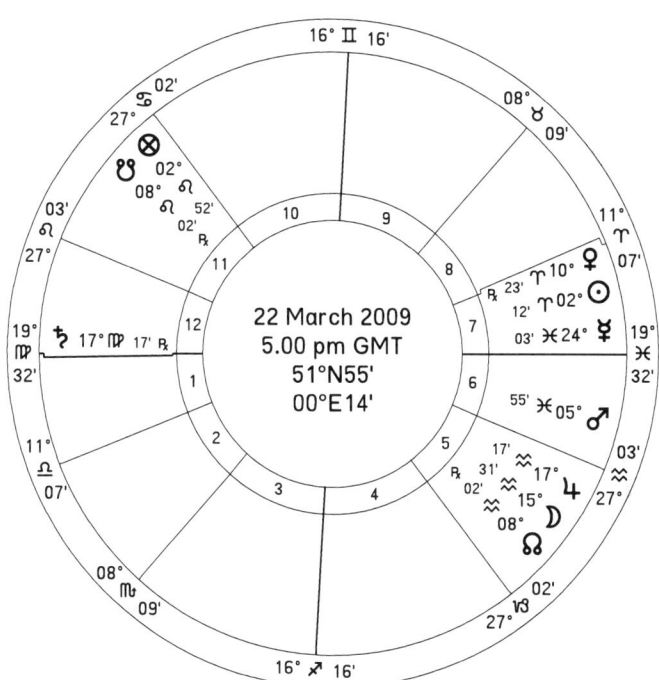

Figure 11.1
JH: 1st body part found.

Jay

Jay's boyfriend returned home to their flat from a weekend trip at about 8 pm GMT on 19 December 2010, but Jay was not at home. He had been trying unsuccessfully to contact her before arriving home, but while awaiting her return he tried to contact her again. This time he heard her mobile ringing and found it in her coat pocket that was also still in the flat along with her purse and keys. He then noticed that their cat appeared to have been neglected. Following a call to Jay's parents, he reported her as missing to the police at 12.45 am GMT on 20 December 2010.

Arrived home
17 December 2010, 8.50 pm GMT
51°N27', 2°W35'

Once the police began their investigation, it became clear through CCTV footage that Jay had reached home on 17 December 2010 at about 8.50 pm GMT after a night out after work with friends. She had bought pizza and beer to take home, and she had clearly arrived home because those items were in the flat. It was on Christmas Day 2010 that her body was found in the snow near Bristol.

From an astrological point of view, the police report is an obvious candidate for its accuracy, but her arrival home – almost a last-seen time – could be helpful. There is another event chart drawn from a much later part of the police investigation which, again, was obtained from CCTV footage.

In the normal course of events, an astrologer's investigations would begin with the first available time, often that of the report, but since there are two

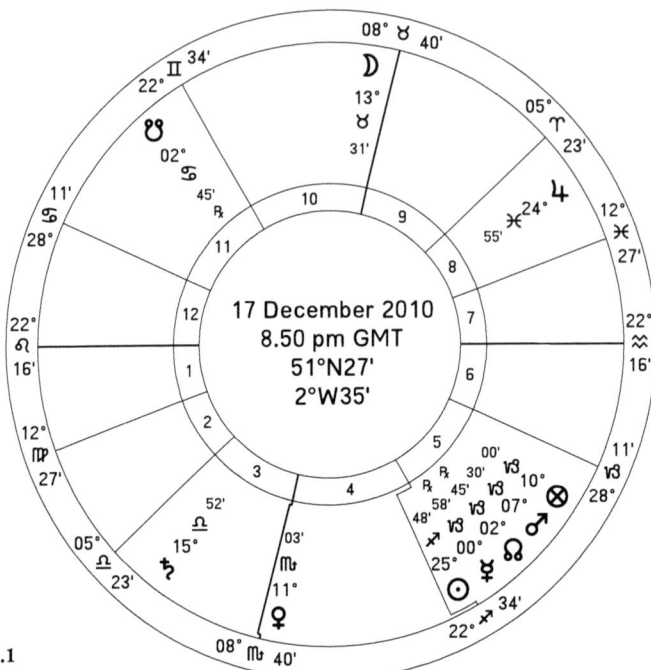

Figure 12.1
Jay: Arrived home.

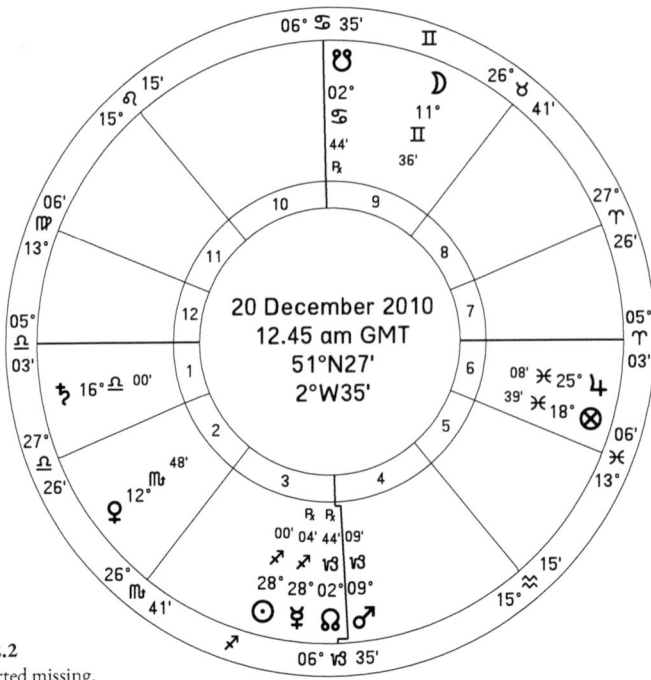

Figure 12.2
Jay: Reported missing.

reliable accounts, we will take them chronologically and start with the time that Jay is assumed to have reached her home. This might provide an 'agenda' for Jay.

The chart has two planets angular: the Moon exalted in Taurus in the 10th, and Venus in detriment in the 4th. Thus, the Moon is public and visible in the 10th, but Venus is private in the more hidden 4th. Taking the Moon as co-significator of Jay, who, then, or what, is Venus that the Moon is opposing?

Jay is signified by the 1st house with Leo rising and therefore she is shown by the Sun which is in Sagittarius in the 5th house of pleasure – she had been enjoying a few hours in a pub with colleagues. Likewise, the Moon is separating from its opposition to Venus – Jay leaving her friends. It applies to a sextile of Jupiter, ruler of the 8th and placed in the 8th. It also rules the 5th and disposits the Sun. Death is in control and it is smiling. The Part of Death at 29°33' Leo is disposited by the Sun, Jay herself, and is the 1st house. Did she have some hand in her own demise? We might also want to consider a motive for death if such it is.

Returning to the earlier question: who is Venus? Detrimented Venus is in Jay's flat; smiling, poisonous Venus. It is tempting to take feminine Venus in a feminine sign as a female, but Venus is oriental of the Sun which adds masculinity to it, and its sign is ruled by masculine Mars. Venus rules the 3rd house of neighbours; Saturn is exalted therein and rules the 7th of assailants. We should also note the Venus-Mars connection again. Mars and Saturn, both exalted, are in square and already connected to this matter: arrogant malice. It seems clear that Jay is not coming home.

Reported missing
20 December 2010, 12.45 am GMT
Coordinates as above

This is the inception of the matter; Jay's boyfriend reported her as missing to the police. So, which is which? Who is the 1st and who the 7th? Indeed, does it matter? Venus, ruler of the 1st, is in detriment in the 2nd house; Mars, ruler of the 7th, is exalted in the 4th. Or, are Jay and her boyfriend both represented by Venus? Saturn in the 1st is indicative of worry, fear, and concern. It is also the natural significator of death. Mars is in the 4th of the grave disposited by Saturn, but could also represent the boyfriend in the flat. In my view,

Jay is described by Venus in Scorpio and this was really only confirmed when her body was found. If she were an angular planet then she would have been nearby or at home, and easier to locate. The lesson to be learnt here is that the descriptions offered by the chart should be given priority in all cases.

Ignoring accidental rulerships, the malefics angular and in square should tell their own story. And we should revisit their exalted condition. Trying to locate Jay at the time of the report is awkward because of the choices offered by the chart. However, there are three arguments for a westerly direction: Libra rising, Saturn in Libra, and the Moon in Gemini. But this does not offer much help; again, we are unlikely to obtain geographical coordinates.

The story is that Jay arrived home with her beer and pizza, but she never had time to eat it. Her attacker, a neighbour in the same building, gained entry to her flat almost as soon as she arrived home. He beat and strangled her and then had to get rid of the body of course. There was no evidence of a sexual assault, but it became clear subsequently that the motive was sexual. He loaded Jay into the boot of his car and then set about establishing an alibi for himself. He went to a supermarket with CCTV and made sure he was seen at 10.25 pm, the time of the following chart.

Murderer shopping
17 December 2010, 10. 25 pm GMT
Coordinates as above

He headed west out of Bristol and stopped at a supermarket at 10.25 pm, that is one hour after Jay is calculated to have died. At this point her body was in the boot of his car. Venus is intercepted in the 3rd house of short journeys still opposed by the Moon of travel exalted. As mentioned, interception, in my opinion, has the sense of enclosure to it. He then proceeded to dump her body at the side of the road some 5 kilometres (3 miles) southwest of her home near the entrance to a quarry. She was found in the snow on Christmas Day by dog walkers.

The murderer had violent pornography, particularly relating to strangling women, on his computer along with indecent images of children. He had subjected Jay to a violent assault lasting some thirty or thirty-five minutes and causing approximately forty-three injuries. The cause of death was strangulation. He was sentenced to twenty years in prison with no parole.

The number of times that the 3rd house arises in these charts should alert us not just to the neighbour, but also to transport. The angularity in these charts is malefic or, at least, worrying. Although the arguments vary somewhat from case to case, the similarities are many in terms of tone and atmosphere.

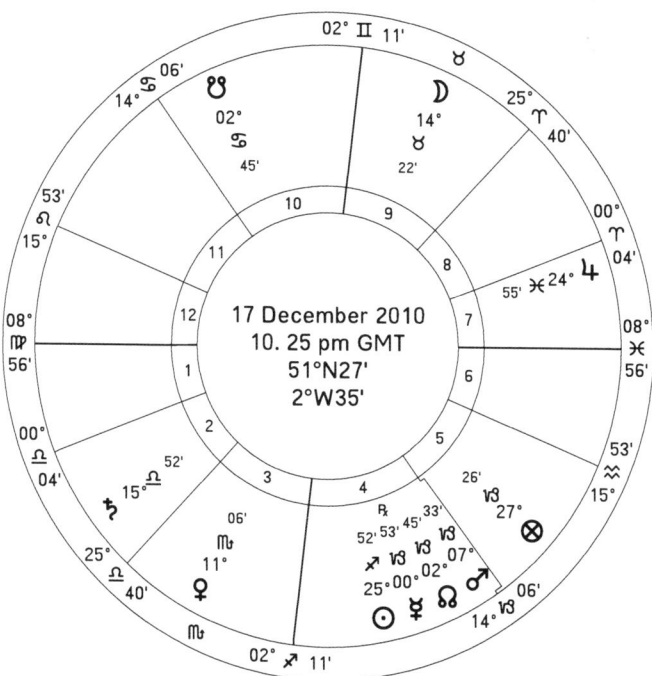

Figure 12.3
Jay: Murderer shopping..

Elle

Mentioned previously, the last-seen time can be useful in cases of abduction or disappearance; the problem is that such a time relies on witnesses for its accuracy. However, in our electronic age, we have the mobile telephone and in this case the last text message sent by the victim. Forensic science has progressed in many different areas and the mobile telephone is just one way in which they can not only date stamp an event, but also locate it geographically. In this case, the text message evidence preceded the report to police by some six hours.

Last text
8 May 2020, 12.49 pm BST
50°N51', 00°W59'

Elle was sixteen years old and had been living with an aunt and husband for about two weeks. She had left her mother's home because of disagreements. There had been rows between Elle and her aunt and the husband was known to have made inappropriate advances to Elle. Elle also had a boyfriend, a relationship described as 'on-off'.

Five planets are angular including her significator, the Sun, and it is very visible in the 10th house. She also appears to be with someone symbolized by Mercury. The Moon is in the 4th but in early Sagittarius; the 5th cusp is at over 28°, so almost the whole sign is intercepted in the 4th. The Moon is associated with messages and transmission so we might consider it as representing her telephone; the means by which she has sent this text message. The Moon separates from a sextile with Saturn, ruler of the 7th house and placed in the 6th house by the 5° rule. It now applies to nothing and so is void of course: the

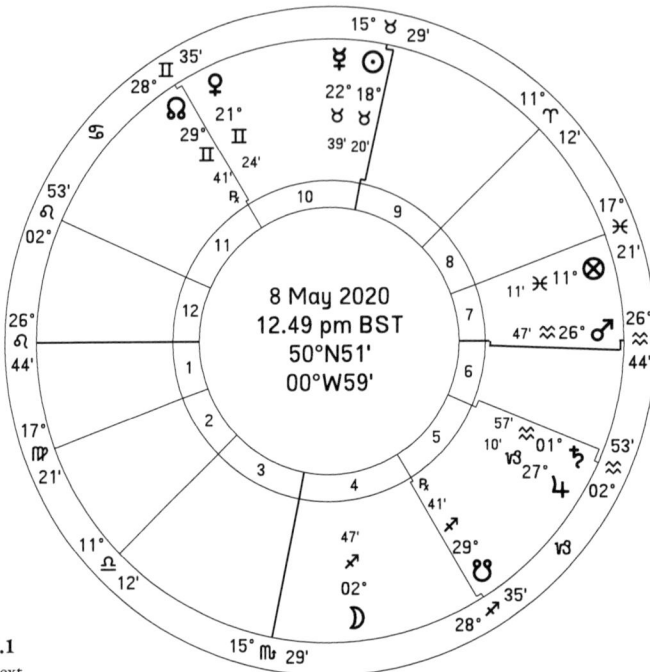

Figure 13.1
Elle: Last text.

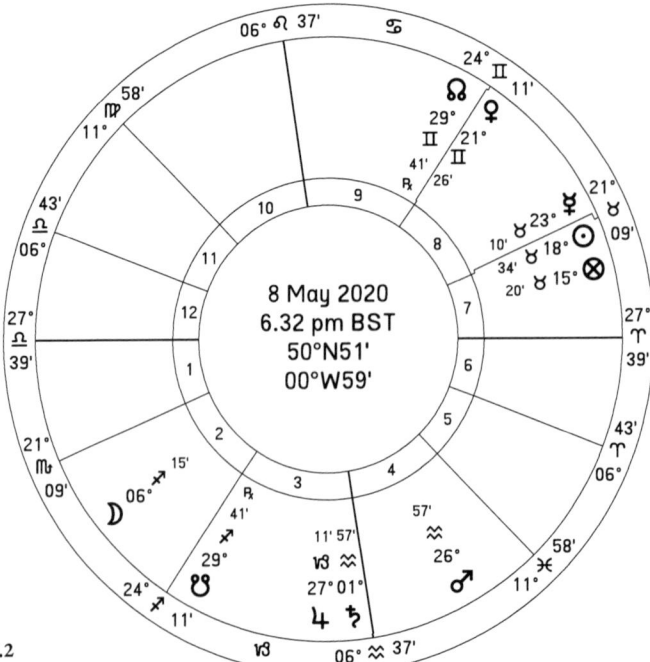

Figure 13.2
Elle: Reported missing.

mobile telephone is 'going nowhere'; it will not be used again. At about 1 pm BST a mast away from Elle's home picks it up.

As in other cases presented here, Mars and Saturn are active: Mars is in the Saturn ruled 7th and is disposited by Saturn. Mars, of course, opposes the Ascendant, the body of Elle. Saturn is in its own sign and house; we might say that this person is at home in that particular location, has strength there. It is a very unfortunate and hidden location being below the horizon and cadent. Mercury is with the Sun and it is in mutual reception with Venus; it rules the 11th of trust and friends. Elle was known to drink alcohol and smoke cannabis, both Venusian, was this the lure? Venus and Mars are active in an appropriate context indicating sex and/or sexual jealousy. Venus in the 10th house and in trine to Mars in the 7th is shouting this very loudly. The Part of Death is at 16°31' Taurus thus Venus gives an indication of the cause of death in the sense of what led up to it. This chart speaks of a sexual motive.

Reported missing
8 May 2020, 6.32 pm BST
Coordinates as above

Her aunt, who had been unable to contact Elle by telephone, made the report to the police. The Ascendant is in late degrees, noting that the previous Ascendant was moving into late degrees. I often regard late degrees as an argument of death. Elle's significator in the previous chart, the Sun, is now in the 8th house of death. Her significator in this figure could be Venus as ruler of the Ascendant, it is in the 9th house by the 5° rule. It remains in a trine aspect with Mars now ruler of the 7th house and significant of the supposed attacker. It maintains its relationship with Saturn, which is here in the 4th house, the grave amongst other things. The Part of Death is at 16°51' Cancer, the Moon remains void of course, which is another argument of death. A fallen Jupiter with its implication of degenerate excess disposits the Moon.

It was some two weeks before her body was found in woodland. She had been subjected to an extremely violent beating with many blows to the head and face; the injuries had been devastating. There was some evidence remaining of a sexual assault. An attempt had been made to destroy the body by fire, which had also been defiled. Because of the damage done by the fire, an exact cause of death was never established.

Suspect seen leaving the woods
8 May 2020, 3.10 pm BST
Coordinates as above

This time is taken from CCTV footage where he is seen leaving the woodland; he was alone.

It is not possible to attribute accidental signification from this chart, it is just some footage from the cameras – he is not of one house or another. So we rely on the planets and their positions and here Mercury rules the 1st and 10th houses, the two major angles. Venus is conjunct the MC and Mercury is in trine to the Ascendant. The Part of Death at 11°25' Gemini is, of course, disposited by Mercury. Mercury and Venus maintain their close relationship through that mutual reception by sign. The attacker was certainly known to her who turned out to be her aunt's husband.

On 21 May, Elle's body was discovered, the police having been told where to look. On 16 November, the attacker admitted killing Elle but to manslaughter not murder. The prosecution refused this and he was tried for murder and received a minimum term in prison of twenty-five years. The trial judge did not find enough evidence of a sexual assault, and, of course, the killer did not admit to it, but it seems to me that these three charts all put Venus and Mars into the frame as a motive.

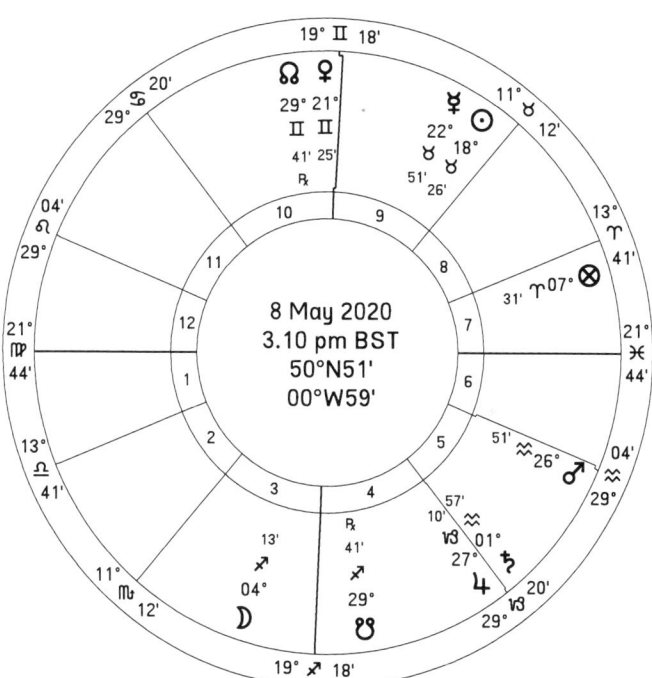

Figure 13.3
Elle: Suspect seen leaving the woods.

GM

Police appealed for information regarding the whereabouts of a two-year-old girl whom they believed had been abducted. They said that they were particularly concerned for the welfare of the chid and mother. It was reported that the child had been abducted from her grandmother's care, that the mother had been staying in a women's refuge, and that there was a restraining order (injunction) against the father of the child.

Last seen approximate time
24 August 2021, 10.00 am BST
54°N03', 2°W48'

Taking Venus for the child as ruler of the rising sign, she is clearly in good health, in no distress, and in full view. Venus mutually separates from Saturn, her father, he is strong by sign and house, has dignity in the 1ˢᵗ, and poses no threat to the child. The mother is the Moon as ruler of the 10ᵗʰ house which is void of course. There appears to be no danger to the child or mother. Venus angular suggests a peaceful conclusion in this case; Saturn dignified is unlikely to harm its own. The other point about that void of course Moon is that the report is of no consequence as mentioned in an earlier case. Although this is not the chart of a report as far as I know (but who reported this time?) we can take note of this since there is little else to focus on. The police knew that the three had boarded an aeroplane bound for Spain.

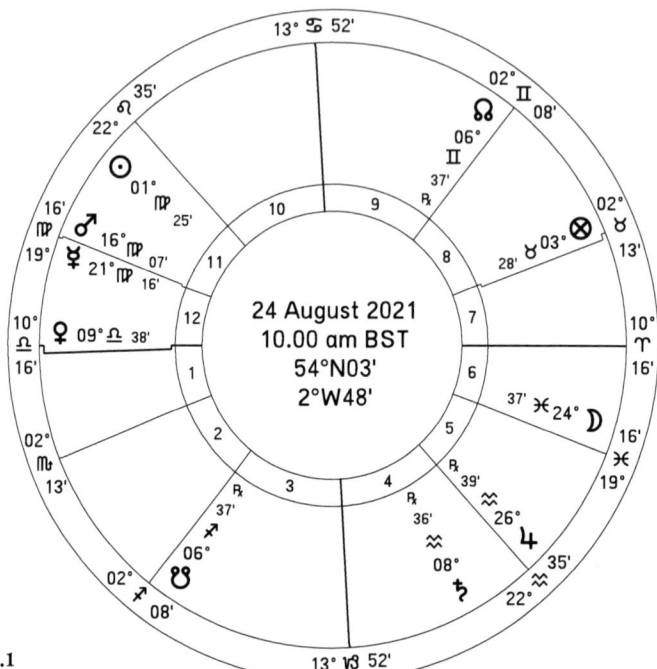

Figure 14.1
GM: Last seen approximate time.

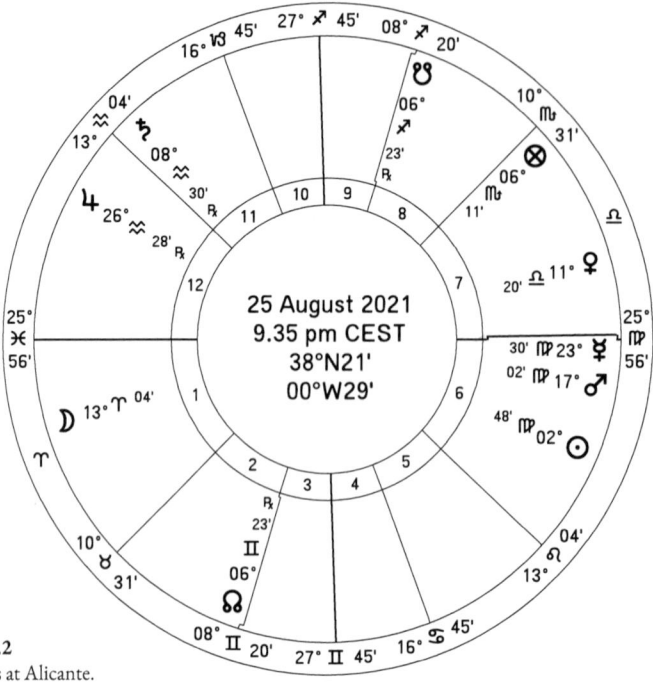

Figure 14.2
GM arrives at Alicante.

GM arrives at Alicante
25 August 2021, 9.35 pm CEST
38°N21', 00°W29'

Moon, Venus, and Mercury are angular, although the Moon and Venus are intercepted. This, of course, could be a concern because of its implication of enclosure and both are void of course. Again there are no apparent threats to the child, and I will continue to use Venus for her. This chart is for the time the flight landed and it seems reasonable to take the 7th house as their destination. This makes Mercury's prominence easier to understand since it rules the 4th of the return home. It is in a wide square with the IC, but retrograde Jupiter is in trine to it. This gave hopes that the child would be returned home. The health and well being of the child seem obvious from the condition and position of Venus.

Two days later the mother and child returned to the UK and the child was taken to a place of safety. No charges were brought against her, but he was arrested when he returned six days later and charged with abduction. At the time of writing, this has not been concluded.

Woman Falls to Death

The woman and her new husband were holidaying in Scotland and were visiting one of Edinburgh's tourist attractions, Arthur's Seat, when she fell the 244 metres (800 feet). Police, ambulance, and fire crews attended the scene but she was pronounced dead at 10.18 pm BST. She was pregnant. Her husband was arrested for her murder two days later.

Emergency services arrive
2 September 2021, 9.00 pm BST
55°N57', 3°W13'

As you will have realized, I like to tell a story and do so in the order of events, but in this case the time is approximate and, surprisingly, there is no angularity. A sign of short ascension rises with Taurus intercepted so caution is needed here. The significations do not seem to tally: the husband as Venus in Libra does not make sense. Even at this stage, he was under suspicion, that it took two days for the arrest to be made speaks only of the gathering of evidence. Even taking the Ascendant for him does not account for the lack of angularity and for the latent position of Saturn ruler of falls. A slightly earlier time would place Venus in the 7th.

Still, working with what is here, Venus is below the horizon showing that she has fallen. The high dignity of her significator is due to her education, she was a solicitor, and she spent much of her spare time working for a homeless charity. She was also an attractive woman who took care of her appearance. That these two planets, Venus and Mars are significators is a sign of sexual jealousy and tension. The Moon will probably remain ruler of the 5th and in the 5th, and it applies to a square of Venus in signs of long ascension and so is equivalent to a sextile. Jupiter is the natural ruler of pregnancy and Venus is in a mutually applying trine with it. Although both are benefics, the Moon will sextile Mars of miscarriage soon. Notice that the Part of Death at 1°30' Cancer is disposited by the Moon, suggesting that the pregnancy was in some way a motive for killing her. There seems little point in taking this further; I wanted to demonstrate how to 'think' about a chart before attempting to judge it.

It was reported by witnesses that he had abused her the day before so this provides some evidence of his character and his lack of respect for her. As Mars is in Virgo, physical cowardice might be expected, but vocally brave.

At the time of writing, he has been charged with her murder and that of the unborn child and he awaits trial, but at the pre-trial hearing he pleaded not guilt to all charges against him.

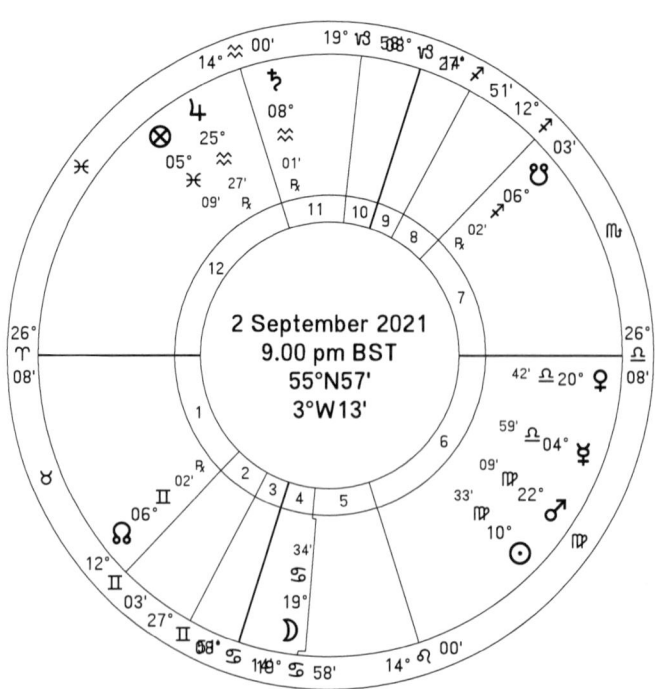

Figure 15.1
Woman Falls to Death: Emergency services arrive.

Woman and Three Children Murdered

Police called to a house
19 September 2021, 7.25 pm BST
53°N23', 1°W30'

The time of the call to the police was later corrected to 7.26 am BST, an ambulance was called at 7.34 am; the caller was not identified in either case. The call to police concerned the safety of a man and they attended four minutes later. The man was arrested at the scene on suspicion of the murders of a woman and her two children, a girl, 11 years old, and a boy, 13 years old, and one of the children's friends, another girl who was also 11 years old. The police statement asked for information relating to 9.30 pm the previous evening to 7.30 am the next day. The man was understood to be the boyfriend of the murdered woman; he had been found sitting under a tree outside the house.

Just as a slightly different approach, here are my notes made at the time that the victims were discovered but before the murderer's name was released.

"Mars as murder indicates stabbing but Jupiter, dispositor of Part of Death [25°26'] Pisces doesn't confirm & Mars in Libra is odd.

21/9/21 Still no cause of death.
Part of Death disposited by Jupiter = drunk.
Jupiter 5th – started on a child, then moved on as mother defended the children.
At least one child was suffocated.
Saturn exalted in Libra, possibly drugs involved.
What happened to him shortly before this? Mars separates combustion?"

The children of the house were killed in their beds and the friend was found outside, having tried to escape. It became clear through the post mortems that the girl living at the house had been raped and then killed. A picture begins to emerge and a very unedifying one.

Mars in Libra is in a strong mutual reception with Venus, ruler of the 1st: the murder and the victim are known to each other. As mentioned elsewhere, in the right context these two planets being significant usually refer to sexual activity or sexual jealousy. Quite clearly, the boyfriend or partner is involved. It is also possible that he made one or both calls to the emergency services. Jupiter, the dispositor of the Part of Death, is in the 5th of children. Jupiter is disposited by Saturn in Aquarius, which is the reason I considered suffocation of at least one child. In light of the rape of the little girl, even though she was ultimately stabbed to death, the chance of suffocation being a factor (hand over the mouth) is fairly high. Saturn is conjunct the 5th cusp but not in the 5th house.

Although I was looking at Saturn as narcotics, it is possible that the 'odd' placing of Mars in Libra refers to recreational drugs and the Moon is applying to the trine of Venus. The 2nd house activity may point to arguments over money in the first instance, possibly for drugs; Mercury is in the 2nd is mutually applying to trine Jupiter in the 5th, already associated with drunkenness. As for Mars separating from combustion, a few months before these murders he pleaded guilty to arson having destroyed a car.

Unfortunately, his trial has been delayed several times; it seems that the court is awaiting the results of medical scans, although there is no explanation for this. The police are convinced that he is the murderer and that suggests that the evidence is incontrovertible, but the alleged murderer has made no plea at the time of writing.

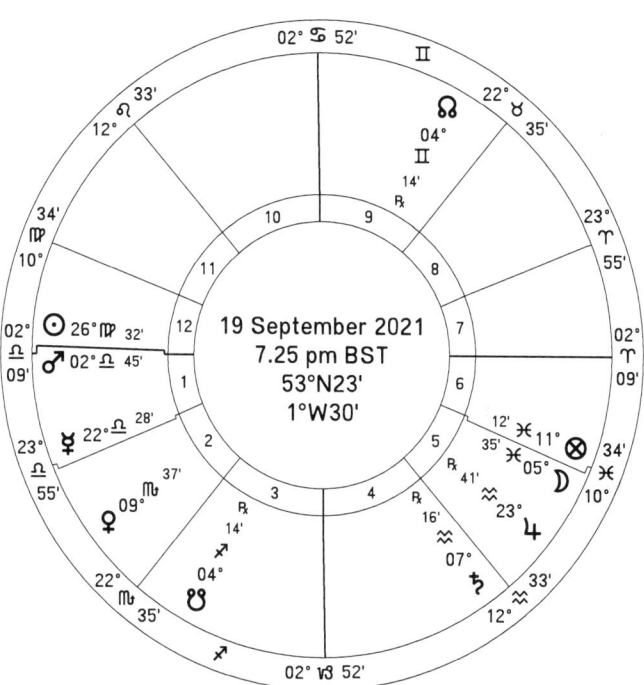

Figure 16.1
Woman and Three Children Murdered: Police called to a house.

CLOSING WORDS

Each of these cases has provided a sometimes-harrowing account of some of the worst crimes that one human being can commit against another, usually against women. I have worked with this kind of material for many years and I have learnt a lot from it: how astrology works of course; how the worst in our society operate; and how the grieving families are often left bereft even of a body to bury. It is for these reasons that I continue to work with such grim events.

The charts do not always provide the answers we might hope for but that is often due to the time used for the chart or charts. Hopefully, with practice and methodical work, we will be reliable enough to persuade hard-headed police officers to pay attention. That day seems a long way off, but we must keep trying to perfect our art.

It should have been very clear throughout this short book that I have consistently used the traditional astrological system and the early modern method that applies it. I have already provided the location of that information should you want it.

You may have found arguments that I have not used or mentioned and that is fine, I do not promote myself as definitive and certainly I am capable of error. But this might prove useful to you as you progress with your own studies.

APPENDIX

Moieties of the Planets
Ptolemy's Table of Essential Dignities

Moieties of the Planets

☉	7½-8½°
☽	6-6½°
☿	3½°
♀	3½-4°
♂	3½-3¾°
♃	4½-6°
♄	4½-5°

Ptolemy's Table of Essential Dignities

Sign	Ruler	Exaltn.	Triplic.	Terms					Faces		
♈	♂	☉ 19	☉D♃N	♃ 0-5	♀ 6-13	☿ 14-20	♂ 21-25	♄ 26-29	♂ 0-9	☉ 10-19	♀ 20-29
♉	♀	☽ 3	♀D☽N	♀ 0-7	☿ 8-14	♃ 15-21	♄ 22-25	♂ 26-29	☿ 0-9	☽ 10-19	♄ 20-29
♊	☿		♄D☿N	☿ 0-6	♃ 7-13	♀ 14-20	♄ 21-24	♂ 25-29	♃ 0-9	♂ 10-19	☉ 20-29
♋	☽	♃ 15	♂D♂N	♂ 0-5	♃ 6-12	☿ 13-19	♀ 20-26	♄ 27-29	♀ 0-9	☿ 10-19	☽ 20-29
♌	☉		☉D♃N	♄ 0-5	☿ 6-12	♀ 13-18	♃ 19-24	♂ 25-29	♄ 0-9	♃ 10-19	♂ 20-29
♍	☿	☿ 15	♀D☽N	☿ 0-6	♀ 7-12	♃ 13-17	♄ 18-23	♂ 24-29	☉ 0-9	♀ 10-19	☿ 20-29
♎	♀	♄ 21	♄D☿N	♄ 0-5	♀ 6-10	♃ 11-18	☿ 19-23	♂ 24-29	☽ 0-9	♄ 10-19	♃ 20-29
♏	♂		♂D♂N	♂ 0-5	♃ 6-13	♀ 14-20	☿ 21-26	♄ 27-29	♂ 0-9	☉ 10-19	♀ 20-29
♐	♃		☉D♃N	♃ 0-7	♀ 8-13	☿ 14-19	♄ 20-24	♂ 25-29	☿ 0-9	☽ 10-19	♄ 20-29
♑	♄	♂ 28	♀D☽N	♀ 0-5	☿ 6-11	♃ 12-18	♂ 19-24	♄ 25-29	♃ 0-9	♂ 10-19	☉ 20-29
♒	♄		♄D☿N	♄ 0-5	☿ 6-11	♀ 12-19	♃ 20-24	♂ 25-29	♀ 0-9	☿ 10-19	☽ 20-29
♓	♃	♀ 27	♂D♂N	♀ 0-7	♃ 8-13	☿ 14-19	♂ 20-25	♄ 26-29	♄ 0-9	♃ 10-19	♂ 20-29

Printed in Great Britain
by Amazon

56926704R00052